PRAISE FOR DIGGER

Digger is an astonishing story, beautifully written, full of suspense, and threaded with the insight and wisdom of the author who has devoted her life to finding the truth of a family secret – whether or not she had a twin. Thrilling, inspiring, and deeply poignant, this is also a story about the search for wholeness, that longing of the heart which is universal.

Words cannot convey the power of this memoir – its dramatic momentum, mystical threads, and profound understanding of human nature and familial relationships. **Digger** is a landmark book, a remarkable achievement which deserves the highest possible recommendation.

OLIVIA AMES HOBLITZELLE
Author of *Ten Thousand Joys & Ten Thousand Sorrows: a Couple's Journey Through Alzheimer's* and *Aging with Wisdom: Reflections, Stories & Teachings.*

In **Digger** Barbara McCollough brings clarity and immediacy to a very complex, layered story. A gifted observer of people in relationships; she knows what they show and what they hide; she knows what they know but refuse to acknowledge. In **Digger** we see how people give themselves away, but of course, what we really see is McCollough giving us these people giving themselves away — through gestures, dialogue, silences — in other words, through ART. Brava!

RICHARD HOFFMAN
Author of *Half the House* and *Love & Fury*.

———

With as much rich compassion as compelling investigation, Barbara McCollough has given us a gorgeously wrought memoir that you won't want to put down, one that you'll never forget.

RACHAEL HERRON
Internationally Bestselling Author of *Splinters of Light*, *A Life in Stitches*, and *Pack Up the Moon*.

To N.K.

PROLOGUE

EVERY SUMMER, NO MATTER WHERE WE LIVED, MY FATHER would pack us all into the car to go visit our relatives in Western Pennsylvania. Much as I was eager to rejoin my cousins to see who had grown the most in the intervening year, to play in the deep green woods and to taste Gram's homemade cinnamon buns which she always made to welcome us, I was most curious to see if Digger was still alive.

Would the black mongrel still be chained to the doghouse just out of reach of the path to Gram's back door, where day after day and year after year he paced at the farthest reach of his tether? Digger would scan the far horizon as though intently on the lookout; he would bark ferociously if anyone came into the yard--or any nearby yard, for that matter. Periodically, he would stop to furiously dig into the earth with a hell-bent frenzy until the chain around his neck suddenly stopped his progress. Even then, he would continue to yank on that chain until he choked, at which point he would capitulate to a power greater than his own. He would pause, and then, seeming to accept his temporary defeat, he would resume his pacing at the chain's farthest extension, his path creating a perfect arc in the front of the doghouse. Years later, when I studied geometry and learned about radius and circumference, I thought of Digger. The path he wore into the earth was as perfect an arc as any that my compass made on the surface of my paper.

My parents would have been surprised to know how much I thought about Digger. The fact was, nobody ever thought about Digger; he was just a dog and no one interacted with him. My grandfather went out and threw a sloppy gruel of leftovers and dog chow into his rusty metal dish once a day. His watering needs were handled by nature; whatever was left by snow or rain or dew in the old upturned hub cap on the perimeter of Digger's walk had to be enough moisture for him. I could tell by looking at the ravaged yard that periodically someone moved the doghouse to give Digger fresh terrain to explore.

What was the purpose of Digger's life, I wondered. Back home in Arkansas, we had a pet dog, Clarence, who was part of our family; he lived in the house with us, even slept in the bed with my younger brother Bill, although my mother put up an obligatory but ineffective protest against this practice.

On one summer visit, I asked my father, "Dad, why is Digger outside by himself all the time?"

"Well, honey, it's because Digger is a hunting dog," my father explained. "Up here, dogs aren't pets. They are used to sniff out the animals when the men go out hunting. That's how the hunter can tell where the animal is."

"Is Pappap a hunter?" I asked.

"No, he doesn't hunt," my father said.

"Isn't Digger his dog?" I asked.

"Yes, he is," my father said.

"If Pappap doesn't hunt, why does he keep a dog for hunting?" I asked. When my father didn't answer, I went on. "If he's not going to hunt, why can't Digger come inside?"

My father was silent.

"Or, if Digger is going to hunt with someone else," I continued, "why can't he come in the house until they go hunting?"

My father sighed. "I don't know. He's not my dog! Why are you asking so many questions? Let's go in for dinner."

———

Two days later I jumped at the chance to help Pappap feed Digger.

"Pappap, why is Digger chained up out here? Can't he come inside the house with us?"

"Naw," he said. "He's a watchdog. How can he do his job if he's inside the house?"

"A watchdog?" I asked.

"Yep, Digger barks like the dickens so we know if some-one's coming," Pappap said.

"But Pappap," I persisted, "He barks even when someone isn't coming, so how do you know when he means it?"

Pappap grunted something I didn't hear and picked up the empty gruel pail. I knew not to press further, but I was confused. Clarence barks from inside the house when someone comes to the door. He didn't need to be tied up outside to do that. Maybe Pappap doesn't know this. Besides, if Digger can't get off his chain, how could he be scary to anyone coming onto the property to do them harm? Only someone stupid enough to go right over to the doghouse.

The more I thought about it, the more uncomfortable I felt with the notion that my grandfather was either dumb not to know a dog could watch the house from inside, or he was so mean he would make a dog stay tied up like that for no good reason. I didn't like either possibility.

"Pappap..." I began again.

"You ask a lot of questions for a little girl," he said, with a mock gruffness which let me know the conversation was over. He turned his back and walked toward the porch.

Throughout the summer, I continued to observe Digger but never again talked about him. I wondered what makes this dog dig so hard? What was he hoping to find? And most importantly, what makes him continue digging despite never finding anything?

One summer when we arrived, Digger was no longer there. A new lawn grew where he had been. No one mentioned him ever again, not even me.

CHAPTER 1

MARCH 13, 1995

DEAR KAYE,

You and I have never met but I have reason to believe we share a very special connection. I believe we may be related and that there are family secrets which have kept us from knowing each other.

I am writing to tell you I plan to visit the Jacksonville area next week, March 23-26, and would very much like to meet with you. I realize this may sound strange and mysterious. I apologize. I'm not trying to be dramatic. The reason for my circumspection will become very clear when we are able to talk in person.

I can understand that you may not want to invite a stranger into your home. May I suggest we make a plan to meet in a public place of your choosing? Please feel free to bring along your husband or a close friend. The nature of our possible connection makes me think it may not be comfortable to bring a parent or sibling. In fact, I would suggest not mentioning this letter or plan to anyone other than your husband or close friend until after we meet.

Although I am not at liberty to disclose full details in this letter, I do want to assure you I am on the level. For this reason, I am writing you on my professional stationery. Please feel free to call and verify that I am who I say I am. Or, if you'd like, you may contact a colleague of mine who can attest to my character and honorable purpose. Her name is Caroline Marvin, Ph.D. She is on the faculty of the Family Institute in Boston and she can be reached at the number listed below.

Would you please let me know at your earliest convenience if sometime during March 23-26 would be possible for you? If not, perhaps I could rearrange my visit to Jacksonville for a more convenient time. I look forward to hearing from you, and hopefully, to meeting you soon.

Very truly yours,

Barbara McCollough

———

I studied the letter to see if I could make it simpler.

I didn't want it to sound too cloak and dagger, but I feared that if I disclosed too much upon first contact, I might scare her away. After twenty years of searching, I didn't want to lose her.

I leaned back in my chair and tried to imagine receiving this letter without knowing what I knew as background information. An eager curiosity immediately sprang forth, but then again, I was always hoping for some surprise to swoop in and change my life.

I read it again. It sounded as if it could be a scam.

"Why?" I asked.

The paragraph about who to bring and who not to bring.

"But it will be in a public place of her choosing!" I argued back.

I sighed. Truth is, I couldn't imagine being in her shoes because I had lived so intensely in my own, treading path after path trying to find her. I would be thrilled to get this letter.

———

At breakfast, I asked my partner Ruth to read the letter. I waited, watching her face as she read. A smile broke out on her face.

"What?! What!?" I asked.

"It's mysterious, no matter what you say," Ruth said. "If she were adopted, she'd think you were either her birth mother or a sister. But since she probably has no idea there is any secret about her birth, I'm sure this will make no sense to her."

"But even if it doesn't make sense, if you got a letter like this, would you respond?" I asked.

"I don't know," she said. "I gotta get to work."

"Thanks a lot," I said as she kissed me on the forehead and headed out the door.

At lunch time, I returned home from the office to take the dog out. As we circled the park, looking for that perfect spot for her to do her business, I consulted with her.

"Scoutie, maybe I shouldn't have mailed that letter."

I looked down to see that Scout, at the sound of her name, had sat down and was looking up at me, cocking her head from one side to the other, listening for a command.

"Good girl," I said, confusing her more, since she had done nothing to earn the praise. I couldn't believe how attached I had become to this puppy. I was not even in the market for a dog. The litter was the product of an accidental mating of a Cocker Spaniel and a Beagle. The little butterscotch and white one snuggled up to my ear and won my heart. When I learned that she had been born on my birthday, our bond was set.

————

At dinner that night, I told Ruth that I mailed the letter but had been obsessing about it all day.

"What do you think? Will she contact Caroline to check me out?"

"Well, would you, if you had gotten this letter?" Ruth asked.

"Yeah, I probably would," I said.

Ruth had become very good in the three years we had been together at listening to my reports of the search, at encouraging me when I was doubtful, at soothing me when I was anxious. I know without her ever saying so that she was sometimes frustrated by my tendency to take three steps forward and then two back. I think she was relieved that I had finally moved out of my mental machinations and into the world of action by sending the letter.

As we cleared the dishes, the phone rang. I froze midstep, plate in hand, until reason reminded me that Kaye couldn't have gotten the letter yet. I put the plate down and picked up the phone.

"Hi, Barb. It's Bill."

"Bill?"

My brother and I had not spoken for six years. He and his then-fiancée had come to Boston to visit. At the end of their visit, we'd had an uncharacteristic and bitter argument during which he and Janine had packed their bags and flown back to California without saying goodbye. In the meantime, they had married and had a daughter who was now around three years old. Hearing his voice on the phone, an empty spot in my heart filled up with sweetness.

He had been the Hansel to my Gretel, and although I was six years older than he, we had been inseparable companions since his birth. Upon hearing his voice, I felt the pain of blood flowing back into a fresh wound.

"I have been thinking of you and want to be in contact," he said. "Life is too short for this to go on. I want Colleen to know her Auntie." He told me he was going to Florida in two weeks to see our parents and wanted to know if I would join them there.

"It's amazing that you called tonight," I said. "Just today I mailed a letter to Kaye Wechsler."

"You're kidding," he said.

"No. Just this morning."

We were silent for a moment, neither of us having to put into words this confirmation that the emotional telepathy we'd always shared was still intact.

"In the letter I proposed that I come to Florida on the twenty-third to meet her." I said.

"Wow."

"Yeah, big wow! So if that happens, maybe I can come on over to Mom and Dad's from there," I said.

My throat closed and despite multiple attempts, I couldn't clear it. It was trying to protect me from saying things I want to feel but don't.

9

I can't believe I even voiced the possibility of meeting Kaye, much less jumping over the six years of silence between Bill and me and going right on for a family visit.

"Let me think about it," I said, backpedaling. We confirmed the dates again and I said I would get back to him when I knew more.

As I hung up the phone, I heard Ruth from the other room, mimicking the sound of the Twilight Zone theme song.

———

The next morning, I woke to dark stillness. It was not only pre-dawn, but pre-Scout, so I was hesitant to move a muscle, knowing that if I did, Scout, who was asleep on my feet, would come to instant readiness to go out regardless of what the clock said. I stretched my eyes, trying to spot the alarm's face without moving my head.

3:15 a.m.

Scout stood and moved toward my head. I wondered if it's awakened consciousness Scout senses, since I have moved only my eyes and my thoughts.

She licked me once on the face and jumped down onto the floor on my side of the bed. I threw back the covers, knowing if I hesitated, she would whimper and wake Ruth. At the bottom of the stairs, she waited expectantly under the hook where her leash hung. For a moment, I considered ways to explain to her that it was much too early to go out-- or too late. I wondered if there was a way to refuse to take her out without provoking a noisy protest, but I saw from the resolute stance of her little body that her mind was made up.

Damn that willful, vocal Beagle side of her nature!

I left the condo door unlocked, but as we stepped out onto the front porch, I patted my jacket pocket to make sure I had my key to the building. I breathed in the crisp night air as we crossed to the park on the opposite side of the street. At this hour, in the glow of the old-fashioned street lights, I appreciated about Brookline what I complained about by day. The ban on overnight parking made for a clean and serene middle of the night, casting the Village in the mode of a timeless small town before cars.

In the moonlight, the letter to Kaye seemed like a dream, but the knot in my gut told me it was real. I found it hard to believe it had been less than twenty-four hours since I sent the letter. At the earliest it would be another twenty-four before it even got to her.

If it got to her. What would she do? Would she call me? Somehow the reality of that possibility, maybe even probability, hadn't sunken in yet. I imagined picking up the phone and hearing a stranger's voice say, "Hello, this is Kaye Wechsler."

Oh my God. Where would I begin? What would I say? Somehow I had imagined walking into a restaurant, spotting her, going to the table and, if she is who I think she is, all would easily play out from there. I hadn't considered the in-between, her calling and inquiring by phone what this is all about, arranging the logistics of meeting. I had sent the letter as though I had an agent arranging it all.

It felt as if I had a weight strapped to my chest. My breath came out as closely connected sighs. I wondered if I could bear this waiting. Twenty years of searching paled in comparison to the specter of waiting out the next ten days.

What would I say, either on the phone or in person?

Even if we met in that fantasy restaurant scene, what would happen afterward? How would we begin to share the stories of our separate lives? Suddenly it occurred to me that, since I'm the only one who has knowledge in advance, I could start by writing out my side of the story.

Back in the condo, as I waited for coffee to perk, I pulled out a pad and pen and on it, I began to tell Kaye the story I have tended in my heart since the day we were born.

CHAPTER 2

MARCH 14, 1995

Dear Kaye,

I mailed a letter to you yesterday and I can't stop thinking about it.

I know it could be several more days at the earliest before I hear from you and I cannot seem to do anything but wait! I can't focus on a book or TV, I can't bring myself to clear out the pantry or rearrange my drawers. The only productive thing I can think of to do is to prepare for meeting you. We're going to have a lifetime to catch up on, so I thought I'd write some of the story down to help get us started once we make contact.

As you probably know from my letterhead, I am a clinical social worker in private practice in Boston. The person I suggested you contact as a reference, Caroline Marvin, was my mentor during my post-graduate training in family therapy.

It is uncharacteristic of me to lead off with my professional identity, and yet it seems appropriate, in that my search for you is inextricably bound with my entering this field in the first place, and what I have learned over the years has steadily increased my determination to find you.

In September of 1975, I moved to Boston for a clinical internship at Massachusetts General Hospital as part of my graduate work at Smith College School for Social Work. Smith has a program which allows you to do coursework in the summer on campus in Northampton, MA and then do a clinical internship at a number of locations throughout the US during the academic year.

At the time, I had hoped to attend Smith for the summer and then be assigned to a small social service agency back home for my internships. I was pretty confident that my request would be granted, for I was the only student in my class from Virginia and there would be no competition. Much to my surprise, Smith assigned me to the highly-coveted Massachusetts General Hospital in Boston. Although a prime placement, I panicked! I knew no one in Boston, and unlike my home area, where I had waitressing jobs, I had no means of supporting myself for a forty-hour a week unpaid internship.

It was a cool September evening, one of my first in Boston. Soon after I arrived, I found an apartment to share with Anne, a school teacher.

On my first Saturday with her, Anne hosted her friend Mark and his fiancée Kim for dinner and she graciously invited me to join them.

The doorbell rang just as Anne had sunk both hands into a bowl of dough.

"I'll get it," I said.

I opened the door.

"Oh!" the woman in the foyer exclaimed. Her face lit up with recognition as she moved toward me with her arms extended, and then stopped abruptly. "Oh, I'm sorry," she said, blushing. "For a second I thought you were someone from home."

"Really?" I smiled at her and the man standing behind her. "You must be Kim and Mark. I'm Barbara, Anne's new roommate."

"Hi, you guys!" Anne's voice interrupted. "Come on into the kitchen. I'm just finishing up."

During dinner, Anne and Mark, who were old friends, entertained Kim and me with tales from their shared past. Kim had seemed a little nervous meeting Anne for the first time and my presence as a fellow newcomer seemed to help her feel at ease; we even joked about being outsiders to Anne and Mark's longstanding and treasured friendship.

The wine and the delicious vegetarian lasagna Anne had prepared added to the pleasant atmosphere and by the end of dinner we all felt like old friends.

Eventually, the conversation turned to Kim and Mark's engagement and their wedding plans.

"It's not easy to plan a wedding when the families are so far apart," Kim said. "Mark's family is all in New England and my whole family is in Florida. Even there they are all spread out. Some are in Tallahassee, some in Miami. Most of them are in Jacksonville where I was raised, so we're going to have the wedding there."

"What a coincidence," I said. "I was born in Jacksonville."

"You're kidding," Kim exclaimed. "What part of Jacksonville are you from?"

"I'm not really from Jacksonville," I said. "I was born in the naval hospital there but my dad got out of the Navy right after I was born and we moved back to my parents' home state of Pennsylvania."

"Too bad you didn't get to stay longer." Kim said. "Florida is a great place to grow up."

"Well," I said, "I can't say my family ever really experienced Florida, or even Jacksonville, for that matter. When you're in the service you experience the service. So I would have to say I am from the Navy, which in my mind is not a great place to hail from."

"What do you mean?" Anne asked.

Suddenly I was embarrassed, as though the wine had danced me out on a limb and I was saying things I didn't necessarily think or feel and had to find my way back from.

"Oh, nothing really," I said. "It's just that from a medical perspective, they seemed pretty disorganized when I was born."

"Really?" Kim asked. "Like what?"

"Let's see," I said, stalling in hopes that an example would float forward. "One time they delivered the babies for feeding time and my mother was the last to get hers. She looked down and said, "This is not my baby."

The nurse insisted it was. Turned out it *wasn't* me. By the time they got me back to my mother, I had nursed from another woman."

"Oh my God," Kim said.

"I don't know what's true about these stories. I don't remember firsthand," I joked. "So I am just going on what my mother told me. They even made a mistake on my birth certificate. It says I am a twin!"

"Whew!" said Anne. "That's a pretty big mistake."

I was feeling a little giddy from the wine and was enjoying the limelight. "As a matter of fact, there's a whole story that goes along with the botched birth certificate. Want to hear it?"

"Sure! I love a good story," said Kim.

"If you insist," I said, feigning a twisted arm. "When my mother was pregnant with me, the Navy doctors were horrible. In her eighth month, my mother was so huge that the doctor on call the day of her check-up told her if she didn't lose weight before her next visit, she'd have to find another doctor. Can you imagine? As though she really had that choice, being in the military. They also told her she either had a baby with a very fast heartbeat or she had two babies in there."

"Or, I suppose," Mark said, "one baby with two hearts."

"Mark, that's grotesque!" Kim said, slapping him on the arm.

"Wait a minute," Anne said. "Are you saying they thought your mother was going to have twins?"

"Yeah, I guess so," I said. "Those were the days before ultrasound, so they had to go on what they picked up with a stethoscope. They thought they heard two heartbeats. Then when my mother went to the hospital to have me, the OB nurses were all worked up about a Mrs. Wechsler, who they thought was going to miscarry. They were worried because this Mrs. Wechsler was kind of frail psychologically-speaking and they were afraid if she lost her baby, it would really send her over the edge."

I paused for a sip of wine.

"My mother remembers waking up in the recovery room after I was born hearing the nurses say Mrs. Wechsler had lost her baby. Although my mother didn't know Mrs. Wechsler, she felt terribly sad for her. Later, when my mother woke up back on the ward, she learned that Mrs. Wechsler hadn't lost her baby after all, because there she was with a baby at her breast. My mother thought maybe she had imagined that she'd heard that Mrs. Wechsler's baby had died, you know, because it had been on her mind and then, being under anesthesia, she thought it was real. Like a drug induced hallucination or something."

"I don't get it, though," Anne said. "Didn't you say your birth certificate says you are a twin?"

"Yes, it does. But my mother didn't know that at the time of my birth. They only received the official birth certificate three months later. By then, my father had been discharged and they had moved back to Pennsylvania."

I felt the silence fall around us. I was embarrassed that the wine had loosened my lips and I had become so engrossed in telling the story that I seemed to have forgotten that these people were near strangers to me.

I looked up from my wine glass into Kim's face. She was staring at me intensely. I thought I saw fear in her face.

"What is it, Kim?" I asked.

Kim sighed. She began to speak, stammered over a few words, then stopped. "Do you remember," she began again, "when we arrived tonight and I mistook you for someone from home?"

I nodded.

"The person you look exactly like is Kaye Wechsler."

CHAPTER 3

MARCH 15, 1995

So there we have it, Kaye.

The night of the fateful dinner party. The Dinner Party, as I have come to call it, the night in 1975 that totally turned my life around. Someone mistook me for you, someone from the same place I was born, with the same surname connected to my birth story that I had known my whole life. And now there was a first name to go along with it, connected to someone who looked exactly like me.

I was shocked. Even though I had had clues in some form my whole life, it never occurred to me that the story of me being a twin was anything other than that--a story.

Since we may be here for a while as I await your response to my letter of March 13th, I'd like to step back and talk about some of the factors which contributed to my search for you and maybe shed some light on why it has taken twenty years! I've come to appreciate that nothing is ever really a straight line, nor is there truly a beginning, other than the Big Bang. So this may seem more like peeling an onion.

———

19

On May 22, 1971, the day after I turned twenty-two, Dad and I stood in the doorway separating the church sanctuary from the vestibule. My father squeezed my hand in his big rough paw as he had done a million times throughout my life. It was his thing. When the first note of Wachut Auf spilled out over us, I took my hand away from his and put it in the crook of his arm. He looked down at me, and for a moment I wasn't sure if the blurred image of his eyes was because of his tears or my own.

As we stepped off into our march, I saw the bouquet of yellow-and-orange-flowered bridesmaid's dresses all aligned on the left and the four men dressed in mint-green tuxes on the right. And there in the center, next to Reverend Carlson, stood Frank in his dress uniform, his gaze toward me, reflecting the awe of this moment neither of us believed would come to pass. During the three-hundred-and-fifty-seven days he'd been in Vietnam, without ever speaking about it, we'd each prepared ourselves to never see each other again. Finally, seeing him there at the altar, I breathed out the breath I hadn't been aware I was still holding.

"...til death do us part," Frank was saying as I arrived back from a mental reverie. I realized I had missed a beat, or many... somewhere. Heat rose up through my solar plexus and filled me with panic. Was I supposed to say something, or had I already said it? I looked to Reverend Carlson and then to Frank for direction.

"You may now kiss the bride," Reverend Carlson said.

Our guests cheered and the next thing I knew, Frank and I were walking back down the aisle together arm-in-arm.

———

At the reception at Fort Belvoir, Frank's Army buddies gathered around him, slapping him on the back and shaking his hand. I stood silently off to the side smiling.

My father joined me. "What's wrong?"

"Nothing's wrong, Dad," I said, forcing my biggest grin.

He looked me in the eye and raised his brow. I started to cry. As my father reached into his pocket for his handkerchief, a colleague of his approached, offering congratulations.

I couldn't bear standing there while others watched me dab my eyes. As I scurried towards the ladies' room, I heard my father explain to his friend, "Oh, it's just nerves, you know. All the excitement."

I locked the door to the bathroom and went to the sink. As I splashed water on my face, I wondered, *Could this be nerves?*

That had been my mother's explanation for everything about me for as long as I can remember. According to her, when I had a birthday party, I'd get so wound up (with excitement, in her view, but clearly anxiety in mine) that I made myself sick and we couldn't have the party, or attend the party if it was someone else's birthday. My parents stopped telling me about such events in advance and just started dressing me up and driving me to the location of the party, inserting a gift into my hands as they ejected me from the car. Pretty soon, I figured this out and started resisting when they pulled out the party dress for me to put on.

I looked in the mirror as I gently dabbed my face dry with toilet tissue, trying not to smudge the fabulous makeup my older sister had applied.

I inspected my face and thought I looked pretty good. I

met my own eyes in the mirror and smiled. "That's it. Nerves. I guess it's just bigger because it's my wedding and happens to be the day after my birthday." As I tossed the used tissue in the barrel and turned to go, a sharp pain ran through my abdomen. I ran to the stalls and made it just in time before upchucking the non-breakfast I hadn't eaten that morning. I stood over the toilet dry heaving.

Once again I was back looking in the mirror. "This is not just nerves," I silently said to myself. "I don't know what it is. Can I go through with this?"

The face in the mirror looked back in horror, saying, "What do you mean, go through with it? You've *gone* through with it... you're married!"

I took a quick glance at the high windows on the opposite side of the bathroom.

"Really?" the inner voice said. "You're thinking you can crawl out the window as you did at a fraternity party when you didn't like your date?"

It's true. I couldn't run. All my relatives, all my friends were out there. I'd be so humiliated, and so would Frank and my family. Besides, what about all the gifts?

I took one last glance in the mirror, fluffed my hair and went right back out to the party.

————

We had been married for two years, and try as I might, the unhappiness which found me on our wedding day hadn't budged despite my best efforts. I took up hobbies, I read self-help books. One night, I had stayed up reading a new one called, "I'm OK, You're OK," long after Frank had gone in to bed. That book helped me see that Frank was OK but

I sure as hell wasn't. There wasn't a single suggestion in that book that gave me hope that the deep sadness which had moved into my body could ever be dislodged. I'd always thought when I got married, that sense of loneliness and not quite belonging I had felt my whole life would disappear, but it had only made it worse. I had tried everything-- distraction, change of attitude, even drinking, but the distress only became worse. I didn't know what to do.

———

That night, as I slipped into bed, Frank woke up.

"Is something wrong?" he'd asked.

It was very uncharacteristic of Frank to inquire about my mood and it caught me off guard.

"I don't think I want to be married anymore," I blurted out. It came out tentative, a plea more than a statement.

A part of me hoped he had the answer, hoped that Frank would turn and soothe me and chase away those bogey men of doubt. I wanted to be wrong about what I had come to think. I wanted him to put his arms around me and tell me that it hurt him to realize how distressed I'd been. I wanted him to ask me how he could make it better. I wanted him to tell me he loved me so much that he couldn't imagine life without me. Any or all of the above could have drawn me back in.

He didn't say anything. He rolled over and went back to sleep.

He didn't speak to me for a month. Apparently my doubt, once expressed, was the fatal blow to any remaining connection between us. I began to feel we'd go on forever in silence if I didn't act.

I gathered my belongings together.

————

The day was so hot I could practically see the heat rising off the black asphalt driveway. I sat on the back stoop waiting for Frank to come home from work.

Was he late or was I just anxious? Traffic could be intense coming out of D.C. on a Friday. It could be another forty-five minutes.

I reached down to the martini sitting beside me on the step. I put my finger inside and swirled it around to make sure it was still cold. Finally, I heard the soft roar of his burgundy Mustang Mach I as it came around the corner.

Frank got out of the car, surprise registering on his face.

"What's this?' he asked in a tone of cautious expectation.

I held out the martini to him.

"Today's the day," I said.

Tears sprang to both of our eyes. I got up and went inside to serve the Alaskan King Crab soufflé I had made. I felt as though I was watching myself in slow motion as I lifted the serving spoon and laboriously dragged it through the air to his dinner plate. I then took a breath and made my way back to the tureen and repeated this feat to deposit food onto my own plate.

I was aware as I held onto each second that this was the last time I would ever be performing this function, in this place, with this person. I knew what was to come after dinner, and although Frank knew something was up, he couldn't know that when we finished eating, I would be cleaning up the dishes and driving out of his life for good.

But he wasn't asking, either. Hadn't he heard me say, "Today is the day?"

As we ate in silence, I pondered the situation. If he had heard me, what did he make of it? I could bring it up, just in case he didn't hear what I'd said or understand.

No, it was too late for that. There was not enough breath in my body to talk over the gap that had grown between us.

After I dried the last dish, I went into the living room, where he was already watching the nightly news, an opened beer on the armrest beside him. I bent down and gave him a quick kiss, an action I had performed a hundred times when I was on my way out to run an errand. The only thing missing was the question from me, "Do you need anything?"

I put my dog Sheba in the packed car and drove off to yoga class, knowing afterward I would be going to my parents' house and not home.

On the way, I called Frank's friend Tom to tell him I'd left, knowing Frank would drink himself into oblivion in front of the TV before he would let anyone know I was gone.

In yoga class, I fell into *sivasanah*, the corpse pose. This was easy, because every part of me felt dead.

What had I just done?

My actions made no sense to me. I knew it wasn't Frank I was leaving. He was a good guy and had always treated me well. It was something in me I couldn't figure out, much less fix.

Kaye, already this is too painful. I can't go through with this. I have to stop.

Oh my God. I must really be losing it. How could this letter feel like a real conversation had been taking place, so much so that I forgot I haven't even sent it? That I don't even know you?

And that, like it or not, everything between us was already in motion, and just like my wedding day in the bathroom, or putting Sheba into the car, it was too late to call it off.

CHAPTER 4

MARCH 16, 1995

HERE I AM AGAIN, KAYE. THERE SEEMS TO BE SOMETHING IN me that has decided to keep doing this until I hear from you. Come hell or high water, my Gram would say.

Could be tomorrow, could be a week from now. Could it be never? I hope not.

————

After I left Frank, I took my dog Sheba and found a new life and a new job. When that wasn't fully satisfying, I made a cross-country trip with a friend. I was operating on the assumption that if I kept active enough or tried hard enough to be interesting or fit in, I would be happy.

One day after returning from my big trip, it suddenly struck me that all of my suffering was inside me, that what I did in the outer world didn't matter, that I would just manage to be miserable in prettier places. It was all in my mind. My misery was caused by what I incessantly thought about. I couldn't change it and I couldn't control it.

I headed to the place I always went when I needed to understand something.

The library.

I spent the better part of a day reading up on the mind and solutions to overactive thinking. The answer I came up with was sobering, but I knew I had to summon all my courage and take action.

I made an appointment with the counseling center in Alexandria, Virginia. I hardly slept the night before. When I got up, I made myself scrambled eggs and, before sitting down at the tiny table for one, I spread the last bit of black raspberry jam Gram had sent me on my one piece of toast. The warmth of the eggs and the sweetness of the dark purple jam filled me with pleasure. As I washed the plate and my empty tea cup, I luxuriated in the bubbles rising from the Joy dish detergent and the warm water. I went into the bedroom where I had laid out my outfit on the bed--a brand new pair of pantyhose, a half-slip and my favorite dress, the navy-and-salmon paisley knit with the long sleeves I'd made myself in a sewing class.

———

Mr. Berkits met me in the waiting room. He smiled and shook my hand and ushered me into his office, where he indicated a chair in which for me to sit. Once we settled, he asked, "What brings you here today?"

"I want a lobotomy," I said.

Mr. Berkits' eyes widened. His lips looked like they didn't know whether to smile or to purse and his eyes narrowed.

"What makes you think you need a lobotomy?" Mr. Berkits asked.

"Well," I said, "I've had trouble with my mind for about two years now. I have no control over what it thinks about. I thought it would be better if I went away on vacation. I just came back from a three-month cross-country trip and it didn't help at all. I can't stand it anymore. I went to the library to see what could make my mind stop and found out a lobotomy severs the connection surgically."

Mr. Berkits watched me carefully as I spoke, probably to see if I was serious. He tapped his pencil on his notepad.

"Don't worry," I said, "I understand the downside. It means I also won't experience happy thoughts either, but at least I won't suffer anymore." I started to cry. Mr. Berkits handed me a tissue and sat quietly as I pressed it over my eyes, trying to make the tears stop.

"We have less drastic ways to help with this problem," he said. "Let's talk so we can see what's best for you. Tell me about your parents."

"Oh, I am over twenty-one so I don't need my parents' permission," I began.

"I realize that," he said. "I just want to know about your background."

I found this highly unusual. Why would he want to know about my parents? I couldn't think of a single thing to say about them--and what would they have to do with me, anyway?

Mr. Berkits waited.

"The only thing I can think of to say is that they are from Western Pennsylvania."

"Oh? Tell me what that means to you," Mr. Berkits prodded.

I paused. This was really difficult. Maybe I should reconsider.

Mr. Berkits waited.

"They are really hardworking people," I said. "They stick together, and are very loyal, but then they talk about everyone behind their backs. They like to keep secrets about themselves but are quick to tell secrets about others."

I stopped. Mr. Berkits was looking at me, his eyebrows raised and a smile on his lips.

"You're right," he said. "My parents are from Western Pennsylvania and that's exactly how they are, as well."

At the end of our time together, Mr. Berkits told me that because I had private insurance, he thought I should see a local psychiatrist, a Dr. Thorpe, who would help me find a path to peace of mind.

Later that day, Dr. Thorpe returned my call.

"I hear you are from Western Pennsylvania," he said, chuckling.

————

Before I go any further, Kaye, I want you to know that after I trained to be a clinical social worker like Mr. Berkits, I learned that my perception of Western Pennsylvanians was an example of projection--something I felt about my own family that I believed was true of all people from Western Pennsylvania, not just my (and apparently Mr. Berkits') parents.

Oh, God. I said all this so you wouldn't be put off Western Pennsylvanians as future family members, but I've still told you something you might find unattractive about me and my family.

Anything I say seems to turn into mental taffy. No wonder twenty-some years ago I was concerned about my uncontrollable thoughts!

CHAPTER 5

FALL 1974

LITTLE DID I KNOW AT THE TIME, MY RACING THOUGHTS and inner turmoil were not merely symptoms to be quelled with the help of psychotherapy, but invitations to the discovery of life beneath the surface of my ordinary existence.

My friend Steve, knowing my distress over my overactive mind, dragged me to a four-day program called Silva Mind Control taught by a man named Ron. It was both eye-opening and lifechanging. In the course, we learned about the different frequencies of the brain and were trained to control them at will. In particular, we learned to enter our *alpha state,* a level slower than our waking consciousness which created a natural relaxation of the mind. As we deepened our training, we were able to use the technique for accelerated learning and improved memory. Most amazing of all, we practiced ESP, usually described as Extra Sensory Perception. But Jose Silva, the creator of the method, called it Effective Sensory Perception. In order to graduate from the program, we had to go into our alpha state and "solve" cases of total strangers presented to us by a partner.

My partner was an older woman named Margaret with whom I felt great affinity. I sensed a loneliness in her. She was well-dressed, had bloodshot eyes and appeared very tense. I wondered if she was an alcoholic. Or perhaps a rich and lonely society matron. We alternated presenting cases to each other. I would go into my alpha state and Margaret would say the name, age and location of a person whose medical status she knew. I'd proceed to scan the person and report the result. On one of the cases, I couldn't get an accurate picture so I came out of alpha.

"I don't know what it is, Margaret," I said. "I'm not getting a clear picture. When I get past his chest, his whole abdominal cavity is empty. Sorry."

Margaret gasped. "That's accurate. He was in a terrible landslide that dragged him down a rocky hill. All of his organs were ripped out of his body. EMT's somehow packed them back in and he is now in intensive care."

And so it went until we had each done ten cases, ostensibly sending healing as we went. We were told the reason we had to do so many was that it would eliminate the tendency of our minds to dismiss our accuracy as chance.

At the end of the weekend, as Margaret and I were about to say goodbye, I said to her, "All week long I kept thinking you remind me of Debbie Reynolds."

"That's funny," she said. "I was thinking you remind me of Mary Tyler Moore."

We laughed. I suggested we exchange information so we could get together for lunch sometime. She gave me her card. It said U.S. House of Representatives. I was embarrassed, knowing my eyes had widened as I read the card and learned Margaret was a Congresswoman. Margaret smiled at me with a sadness in her bloodshot eyes.

We both knew in that moment we wouldn't be having lunch, but I also felt how nice it must have been for her to be just a regular person taking a workshop. I learned she had taken the course to increase learning and memory for the reams of information passing over her desk daily (hence the bloodshot eyes). What neither of us knew then is that our paths would cross again much later, that I would go to graduate school in Massachusetts and would fulfill the requirement to do my community practice project by becoming a constituent caseworker in her home district office outside of Boston.

———

A few months after the Silva Mind Control course ended, Ron called to invite me to an evening with a holy man from India which was being sponsored by Erhard Seminars Training. I was registered for the upcoming EST training and Ron thought I would enjoy this evening program in advance of the longer training.

I accepted, not because I was interested in meeting such a figure, but because it was Ron, the very charming, handsome Ron, who was inviting me. Never would I have imagined it was Baba, the little holy man who waddled out onto the stage that night, who would be the one to sweep me off my feet.

Before I knew it, I had signed up for a five-day meditation retreat with Baba at the 4H Center in Bethesda over Thanksgiving. It was unfathomable to my parents that I had returned from a trip to Vermont, not to have Thanksgiving with the relatives, but to go and meditate for the entire holiday weekend. My mother offered to put off the turkey dinner until Sunday, when I would be returning to them, but I said she shouldn't bother, because I was now a vegetarian and wouldn't be eating turkey. When I told my boyfriend Dave (the alternate groom who had caught the garter at my wedding) I was also celibate, he nodded his cool shaggy head and said, "Oh, I get it. No meat of any kind." I was so intrigued by what lay ahead, I didn't mind being the butt of others' jokes.

Baba was a shaktipat guru, which means he had the power to awaken the kundalini, the inner spiritual energy of a seeker. The kundalini energy is described as a coiled serpent that sits at the base of the spine. It has two forms: one is the life force which animates our physical bodies and the second is the intelligence, the consciousness which animates our minds and spirits. Once awakened by shakti-pat, the touch of a master, this kundalini energy travels up the spine to the crown of the head. This energy is all-know-ing--it purifies, awakens, destroys and creates and the experience is unique to each individual. From what I heard from Baba's followers, receiving shaktipat transformed lives in surprising, unpredictable ways.

The sixty of us began each day of the retreat with an early morning meditation with Baba. As we meditated sitting cross-legged on the floor, he would pass up and down the aisles, the soft velvety thud of his slippered footfall, the quiet rustle of his silk clothing and occasionally the waft of his fragrant peacock feathers the only audible sounds.

Every morning, as Baba came upon me, he pressed his thumb between my eyebrows and a flood of light burst into my brain like fireworks. I marveled at the experience, thinking, "Oh, wow! He must be touching my optic nerve. What a great trick!"

Baba did this to me four mornings in a row. I thought this was what he did to everyone as he went by, but at meals, I heard others speaking of their experiences. Sometimes he wafted them with his feathers, sometimes he put a hand on their head, sometimes he caressed their faces. I thought perhaps he did certain things to certain parts of the room, but then I realized I sat in a different location each day and yet he did the exact same thing to me each time he passed.

What could this mean, this pressing of his thumb between my eyebrows?

On the fifth morning, as we meditated, Baba did not come in. I grew restless. I got up and left the room (if I am totally truthful, I'd have to say I probably went out to smoke a cigarette). I was standing in the hallway near the auditorium door when I heard a shushing kind of commotion.

I looked up to see Baba walking right for me, his entourage at his back. When he got to me, he grunted and made an upward motion. One of his aides said, "He wants you to open your hand."

I did so and Baba popped a warm fritter into my palm. In that moment, I remembered that Baba liked to cook. I recognized this was a very special moment and I was being given *prasad*, blessed food.

My mind went wild, thinking, "Oh my God, this would be very special to one of his followers in the room. Too bad he is wasting it on me, a mere visitor."

Baba grunted again, waiting. This time I knew what he was indicating and I popped the fritter into my mouth. I felt the warmth of it all the way down, from my lips to my throat, to my chest, into my stomach and beyond.

Baba grunted again, turned and went into the meditation hall.

———

Two months later, I applied to graduate school, and within six months, I had moved from Virginia to Massachusetts to attend Smith College School for Social Work.

Before a year had passed, I was in Boston, Kim mistook me for you, and you know the rest of that story. It is hard for me to recount that part of my history without wondering if having my kundalini energy awakened by Baba played a role in all the events leading up to The Dinner Party.

CHAPTER 6

MARCH 17, 1995

Happy St. Patrick's Day, Kaye.

I wonder if you know you might be Scotch/Irish?

I am getting a little nervous that I haven't heard from you. I wonder if the letter actually got to you? If it did, are you ignoring it? Or did your response get lost? It helps me to tamp down my over-thinking to just keep on writing.

When I woke up the morning after The Dinner Party in 1975, I had an immediate awareness that something was totally different about my life, but I couldn't place what it was.

Oh. Right. Last night. I look just like Kaye Wechsler.

My cheeks grew hot. My throat tightened. My face felt as though someone had torn off my cheery mask and exposed my true face—a face which felt raw, totally foreign and yet familiar. Without warning, I had been thrown into the abyss above which I had spent my entire life dangling, the one which, even as I hung there, I had convinced myself did not really exist.

How could I look exactly like Kaye Wechsler from Jacksonville, Florida?

It was absurd. Yes, I had known the Wechsler story and the birth certificate story. They were just stories, like other childhood stories I loved but knew were not real. Now it was as if someone had said, "The Velveteen Rabbit? Yeah, I grew up with him."

This isn't true, I thought. *I know I can't possibly have a twin. It's a tall tale that has gone on way too long.*

I got out of bed and went to the desk. I pulled out a piece of paper and wrote *Bureau of Vital Statistics, Jacksonville, Florida* in the upper left.

Dear Sir or Madam,
 I am interested in obtaining a copy of my birth certificate.

I filled in the particulars. I licked the edge of the envelope flap decisively, as though I was sealing up the question itself and sending it away where it would have no power to intrude on my new life. My stomach let go of its grip on my breath as I imagined the relief of learning there was nothing on my birth certificate to indicate that the story my mother had told me was true.

———

The following Monday morning I began my second week in the clinic. As I bobbed along on the subway to the Charles Street stop, I saw my reflection in the window. I looked older than I had last week, with a much more somber look about me. I could tell by the look on Carmela's face that there had been something different in my response to the outpatient secretary's jovial greeting.

"Bad weekend?" she asked.

I murmured something about being tired and went down the hall to my little cubicle of an office and shut the door.

I'm not going to be able to do this. I don't even know these people yet. I can't tell anyone what happened. But worse, I can't seem to act my normal self.

I had already been nervous about seeing my first clinical patient. I'd read the case history and panicked. What could I possibly do or say to be helpful? All the course work I'd had in advance of this internship had evaporated. I felt like a fraud, no more qualified to be sitting with clients than a person off the streets. And now, my ability to pretend I knew what I was doing had left me.

I opened my first patient's chart. Despite my best effort to focus on the task at hand, my mind kept returning to the thoughts that had preoccupied me all day Sunday.

I can't tell anyone about what happened at The Dinner Party.

Actually, I can't tell my parents about it, and therefore I can't tell anyone.

I tried to envision talking to my mother, but no image entered my imagination. If there was any possibility the story about Kaye Wechsler was true, it would blow my family apart. It would change everything. We couldn't just set another place at the table as if she'd been there all along.

I don't want anything to change.

I closed the chart and stood up, hoping I could shock my mind back to the present. A wave of nausea overtook me.

Whether I told anyone or not, everything inside me was changing. I was not the same person who'd arrived in Boston last week and I didn't know how to be anyone else.

Not only could I not imagine speaking to my parents about it, I couldn't imagine meeting you, Kaye. I couldn't imagine anything. I was numb.

"It's all probably nothing," I told myself. "You are making a mountain out of a molehill." I tried to calm myself. "When the birth certificate comes, it will put everything to rest."

Three weeks later, when I arrived home from the clinic, I stopped at the phone table in the vestibule. I checked for telephone messages and then reached for the stack of mail beside the phone. A bill from Visa, a letter from my mother.

An envelope from the State of Florida.

I shuffled it under the other two envelopes and went into the kitchen for a Diet Coke. I exchanged a few words with Anne about her day, I hung up my coat and then went into my bedroom. After I took off my skirt and hung it up, I put on my jeans. I sat down on the edge of the bed and drew the Florida envelope out from under the stack. For a moment, I sat staring at the official type.

You don't have to open it, a voice inside said.

Oh, don't be ridiculous! You are being so dramatic, another voice answered.

I tore the end of the envelope and pulled out the letter. Enclosed in the eight-and-a-half-by-eleven paper was a smaller paper, maybe four-by-six, a dark photostat of the original.

My eyes scanned down the page; past the name, date and name of parents until they landed on a checked box.

Twin birth.

I froze, staring for a timeless moment at the page, unable to think or to move. And then I opened my desk drawer, placed the paper neatly under my *Things to Do* notebook and went out to the kitchen to help Anne with dinner.

CHAPTER 7

FALL 1975

ONE EVENING, ANNE HELD OUT A FLYER.

"This sounds like fun. Want to go with me?"

It was an invitation to a Fall mixer at the Harvard Club. It did look like fun.

"But I didn't go to Harvard...?"

"No matter," Anne said. "You can come as my guest. A great place to meet someone."

Meet someone? I was so taken up with my new life, first at Smith and then at MGH, a social life was the last thing on my mind.

Truth be told, the reason dating was not on the list of things I'd recently thought about was that I wasn't as unattached as I'd allowed my new acquaintances in Boston to believe. Although I had been separated from Frank for more than a year, my divorce was not final. It wasn't exactly that I was hiding that fact, but it had been a painful period in my life and I wanted a fresh start.

"Okay," I said. "Sounds good."

We entered the impressive gray granite building on the

corner of Commonwealth and Massachusetts Avenues. I had not been out at night for a social reason since I'd moved to Boston. The city had the same exciting buzz to me that Washington D.C. had had and yet was very different.

Or maybe I was different. I was beginning to feel grown-up, able to make my own decisions, presenting myself in a new form. Even though I felt like an imposter, I was proud to say I was a Smith student doing a clinical internship at Massachusetts General Hospital. It was exciting to put on that new identity and see what happened that was different from being a wife and daughter in Virginia.

Nick approached me the moment I stepped away from the coat check and asked if he could get me drink.

"He's cute," I thought. I accepted his offer, and while he was gone fetching the drink, I took stock. I felt awkward. What should I say now?

Nick came back with the drinks and as *Rock Your Baby* started to play, he took me by the hand and lead me to the dance floor. Dancing was a relief, giving me time to observe him and to calm my own mind in the privacy of the blaring music. By the end of the evening, I'd learned that Nick had a Ph.D. in mathematics from Harvard, was divorced and had two children. We both loved playing the piano. I stopped taking lessons when I hit junior high, while Nick was a virtuoso who played concerts.

"How about a squash game?" he asked at the end of the night.

The expression on my face must have let him know I had no idea what he was talking about.

"It's a game like badminton, but you play it inside with a hard rubber ball."

"Ok," I said.

Thus began a relationship which lasted almost two years. I was fascinated that someone could actually be that smart, had a mind which seemed to be thinking really heady thoughts all the time like a walking encyclopedia.

Yet he was also a passionate, accomplished pianist. The music he played for me excited my body as much as his theories on everything stimulated my mind. And yet, much as I wanted this new relationship to work, it was as if it was one more piece in the dollhouse I was creating in my mind. I wasn't really in the picture. Like my marriage to Frank, it was another scenario which didn't seem to have much to do with me.

One night over dinner at the very start of our relationship, Nick asked me if I grew up in a religion.

His question took me by surprise. This topic rarely crossed my mind.

"I would never say my family was religious, but we went to church when it made sense," I said

"Made sense?" he asked.

"Yeah. I was going to say we went for special occasions, but that wasn't really true."

"When you did go, what religion did you follow?" he asked, restating his question in another way.

I felt uncomfortable with him digging into something so personal. Mostly, I dreaded allowing him to see how unexamined this aspect of my life was.

"I'd have to say we went to the Church of the Proximity," I said. "We moved around a lot, so we went to whichever church was nearby. Lutheran, Methodist, Baptist, Congregationalist. When I was the appropriate age to be confirmed, we happened to be going to a Lutheran church in Virginia."

He laughed. I felt bad after I'd said that because in fact, my parents were married in a Lutheran church and I'm sure that influenced their choice of churches when we settled in Virginia. But I didn't want to get into it, so I just let my flip answer stand.

"You should get down on your knees and thank God you were not raised Catholic," he said.

Nick went on to tell me he was a devout atheist. He had been raised Catholic and rejected the Church's teachings as a teenager. He viewed early religious education as a form of intellectual abuse of children and had become a follower of Madalyn Murray O'Hair, an activist who supported the separation of church and state and was responsible for the Supreme Court ruling outlawing compulsory prayer in public schools.

"She founded the American Atheist Association. I have them in my will."

Wow. Interesting. I'd never met an atheist, much less one who was so vocal and passionate about it.

Listening to Nick made me think of my soon-to-be ex-husband Frank. When we were engaged and he'd returned from Vietnam, I'd insisted he be baptized at St. Mark's, the Lutheran church where I was confirmed. I had put on a full-court press, saying, "You know, Frank, the Bible says, 'He who believeth and is baptized shall be saved.' Who knows what's true. Let's just cover the bases and get you baptized."

Reverend Carlson had baptized Frank in front of the whole community. Poor shell-shocked Frank, through his year in Vietnam must have come to his own relationship with his Maker. When I came to my senses, I felt ashamed at how I had put Frank through a needless charade.

I neglected to tell Nick about my experience getting Frank baptized. I'm not sure if it was because I didn't want to expose my own religious history for scrutiny or if I didn't want to talk about my marriage.

I don't think I told him much about my private self. Come to think of it, I don't think I even mentioned in the whole two years we were together that I had recently discovered I might have a twin I had never met.

CHAPTER 8

MARCH 18, 1995

You may get the letter today!

I am surprisingly calm this morning, perhaps because I am feeling well-loved and supported by my friends who know I'm awaiting word. Carey said it's like waiting for a pregnant friend to go into labor.

She's right. I'm compiling a list of people to be notified when I hear from you. I should start packing my bag for the flight coming up on the 23rd, just as I would if I were anticipating a trip to the hospital.

I had coffee with Diane yesterday.

"I think you'll hear from a lawyer first," she said.

"You're kidding," I said. "You've been listening to too much of the O.J. trial."

It never occurred to me that there might be legal matters involved. What? Is it against the law to try to find your own twin sister?

I can see the patterns in my search over a period of years when I would do something on the outer plane, like sending off for my birth certificate, and then I would disconnect, as though I needed time to digest the reality that I could really have a twin.

Over the years, as I have told my story to new acquaintances, invariably they are shocked that the morning after The Dinner Party, I didn't run to the phone and call information for your number. During that initial six-month period after I got my birth certificate, I wasn't ready to talk to my parents about it, so I didn't talk to anyone.

————

After the 1975-76 academic year in Boston, I returned to Northampton for the second summer at Smith. My parents planned to visit and I knew it would be the right time to talk with them about you. I decided to approach the conversation under the guise of asking them to participate in a family history project. I knew they'd be happy to help me with that.

The day was hot for Northampton. Although the floor-to-ceiling windows facing the park were open in their widest invitational gesture, their gauzy curtains, usually rustled by a whisper, hung still. I sat on the day bed in the living room of my apartment watching out over Elm Street, hoping to see my father as he returned from his errand.

I looked at my watch. It was already 10:30 a.m. I had hoped to be well into the interview with him by now. I sighed. Other than waiting to get started, I didn't mind waiting for my dad. Much of my childhood had been spent waiting for the sound of his key in the lock, when my heart would swell with joy and I would go running at the head of the pack to jump into his arms. My earliest memories of him are waiting. For my first six years, he worked full-time and went to night school, so unless I could wait up late to hear him come in, I only saw him on the weekend.

———

I lay on the couch, the nubby fabric scratching me through my cotton pajamas. I forced myself to endure the itching. I knew if I moved around too much or complained about the scratchy couch I would be sent back upstairs. I watched the man on the TV. He sat at a desk talking to people who were sitting nearby in living room chairs. Every now and then, they would laugh and my mother would laugh right along with them. That made me feel happy, too. I enjoyed watching her face as she laughed--her eyes brightened and she'd let out a little short burst of sound. Sometimes, if something was particularly funny, she would let out a shriek of glee accompanied by an emphatic hand gesture, maybe even a stomp of her feet. But this night, she was just quietly laughing, little crinkles in the corners of her eyes and a smile on her lips. My mother's smile was a special treat. When it was there, the world seemed a cozy place.

I wakened to the feeling of movement. At first I thought I was dreaming, then realized I was being carried. I felt Daddy's strong arms under my back and knees. The coolness of the night air, still lingering on his jacket, refreshed my hot cheek as I pressed it against his chest. I felt each step, each rhythmic bobbing of my body, as though I was on a rubber float upon the ocean waves. The rhythm shifted as he started up the stairs. I saddened as I realized this trip was about to end. He gently released my body into the soft support of the waiting bed, pulled the blanket up to my chin and kissed me on the forehead.

"Goodnight, Daddy. I love you." I said as he started to move away. I waited for him to say his part of our goodnight ritual, but all I heard was his footsteps as he started back down the stairs.

————

I heard my mother putting dishes away in my small kitchen. I wondered what she would do while I interviewed my father. It had never occurred to me to speak with each of them separately, but when I asked them if I could interview them for my family history project, my father jumped right in saying, "I'll go first!" The relief I felt when he spoke made me realize that talking to him first would make my task much easier.

My mother stepped into the living room. "Still out seeing Duncan, is he?" I noticed the Western Pennsylvania inflection in my mother's question, that particular way of going up a beat just before the commonly accentuated syllable.

My friends had chided me over the years about the emphasis I placed on certain words and about the odd cadence of my questions. It wasn't until I heard my parents each time they visited that I could see what they meant. "As we drove in last night, we saw you had a new one."

"Oh no, he's on an errand, Mom!" I said, making air quotes with my fingers. My father had had a Dunkin' Donuts addiction for as long as I could remember, maybe for as long as Dunkin' Donuts had existed. He was constitutionally unable to pass a Dunkin' Donuts without stopping. The first few years it had been a family joke in which he'd participated with good humor. Then he became defensive about his habit and often secretive.

"Why couldn't he just say I'm going to Dunkin' Donuts before we start?" I asked.

And why have we gone along with his little white lies all these years when it was so obvious, I wondered to myself. *Is this his way of dealing with his nervousness about the interview?*

Even though he was quick to volunteer, I didn't for a minute believe he would be all that comfortable talking about his past. If it was easy, I would already know the history. It would have been woven throughout my lifetime, rather than delivered in little whispered snatches by my mother.

"I'm going for a walk," Mom said. "I'll keep an eye out for your dad, and if I see him, I will tell him it's time to make the donuts."

I laughed. "Isn't that ironic?" I said, "that a Dunkin' Donuts addict is the spitting image of that guy? Honestly, every time I see that commercial, I look really close to make sure it's not Dad! Have a nice walk, Mom."

I felt a twinge of guilt that I had not been entirely honest with my parents about the reason for the interviews. I had told them that all psychotherapy trainees were required to construct a detailed family tree, which was true. What they didn't know was that I wanted detailed information about my own birth. Nor could they have known any nervousness they sensed in me was not about being a neophyte interviewer, but about what I might uncover.

———

I heard my father's footfall on the top-floor landing and scurried to the door to open it for him. There he was, filling the doorway even as I opened it, out of breath, his face full of hopeful innocence.

"Hey!" he said, grinning from ear-to-ear. "While I was out, I found a Dunkin Donuts. I didn't realize you have one right here in Northampton." He stepped across the threshold, extending the white, pink and orange bag in my direction. "Got you a cup...decaf, right?"

He unloaded the contents of his bag on the lobster-trap coffee table. "I also got you a Boston Creme..." He stopped when he noticed my crinkled nose. "If you don't want it, I'll eat it."

I watched him settle into the one moderately comfortable chair in the living room, the big white vinyl overstuffed one with a huge split in the right arm. He leaned forward, stretching over his belly to smooth the bag and put the two Boston Crème donuts side by side on it. Then he placed the decaf near me and the regular in front of himself. As I watched his enjoyment in this simple moment, his obvious anticipation of a chat with me, I wanted to forget about all that had plagued me for the past year in order to lock in time the sweetness of our special connection.

I reached over and picked up the Boston Creme donut.

My father smiled. "Atta girl!"

He tore a hunk out of his donut and after a few bites he reached for a wad of napkins and made a pass at the right corner of his mouth.

"Hey, Barb," he said, winking as he took the next bite. "Is that your handiwork?" He nodded his head in the direction of the wall behind me.

I turned to look at what he was referring to and saw on the shelf the stuffed koala bear my friend Kristen had brought me back from Australia.

I laughed. "Yeah, Dad, didn't I tell you about my expedition to the Outback? I also have a stuffed wallaby in my bedroom."

"Yeah, for a while there you had me going, Barb," he said. "I thought you were going to grow up to be a taxidermist."

I gave him a puzzled look. "Oh." I nodded, smiling as I remembered. "Because of Buzzy. That was a riot. I can't believe we stuffed a squirrel."

As I watched my father eat his donut and drink his coffee, I felt warmed by this memory of Buzzy, from a long time ago when my father so readily joined me in doing a project I'd proposed for science class.

Maybe this quest to learn the truth of the birth certificate won't be nearly as difficult as I'd made it out to be. I thought.

"That was really great, Dad," I said. "Of course, I never told the class how much you helped me. Couldn't have done it without you!"

We laughed and raised our Styrofoam cups to each other.

"Or maybe you would have become an undertaker. You were really into dead things," he teased.

It took me a moment to understand. "Oh," I said, "You mean the bird funerals?"

"Yeah, I'm glad you ended up helping live people. You were always so thoughtful of others."

I paused and sipped my coffee. I knew he had rewritten history with a bias toward seeing me as an altruistic, giving person, the way he had trained me to be--solicitous of others' feelings, especially his.

"I remember when you were about four. Your mother and I were separated...you knew we were separated for a while?"

I did *not* know this and was shocked to hear it.

"Well, during our separation I lived with my mother, your Gramma, and you and Joyce would come over to visit on the weekend."

Suddenly I remembered a story I'd been told so often it felt like a memory, of how, when I was four, when it was time for us to leave, my father would sit on the stairs at his mother's house buttoning up my coat, tears running down his cheeks. Reportedly, I had reached out and wiped away his tears and said, "Don't cry, Daddy. We'll come back."

We'd all been separated! Why didn't I remember that? That's why we'd been at Gramma's and he'd been crying as we got ready to go.

As I finished the last bite of my Boston Creme donut, I noticed my heart was beating fast. I wasn't sure I had the fortitude to follow through with my plan, to carefully and calmly cover his history until we reached the period of my birth without getting hijacked into both his and my own reveries of idyllic times past. It was clear my father was really enjoying this opportunity to reminisce. It would be so easy to just go along with wherever he wanted to take us.

But I was on a mission. I reminded myself that this was a rare opportunity, perhaps the only one remaining, where I might get my father to speak with me about his life. A family that traded in secrets, it was hard to keep track of what I'd actually heard from the horse's mouth, which stories I was allowed to know and which should only be referred to behind someone's back. At the very least, the interview would create a new baseline for future conversations.

I had to press on.

"Tell me about your childhood, Dad," I said.

My father smiled nervously as he settled back into the chair, cradling the coffee mug between his hands. "I don't know if you know this," he began. "Grandma had me before she was married. Gus wasn't my real dad."

This I did know, and I also knew it was on the list of things he wasn't supposed to know I knew.

"I was five years old when my mother married Gus. When I was little, we lived with Grandma Thompson, my mother's mother. When Gus came along, we moved out to Ridge Avenue, and then all the other kids started coming. First there was Peg, then Trudy, Judy, Don, Donna and Kathy. I was already out of the house by the time the last three were born.

"Gus? At first he was Okay, I guess, but then he got kinda mean. But he had his good points. ...Oh yeah, that whole deal about the name. That was pretty weird. Gus never adopted me, so I was the only one who had the last name of Thompson. It bothered me that everybody else in the family had the same last name except me. Just before I went into the fourth grade, the family moved to Seventh Street, which meant we had to change schools. Since nobody knew me there as Billy Thompson, I went to school that first day and said my name was Billy McCollough. Just like that! I didn't think much about it until the first report card came out. I felt so proud to see *Billy McCollough* all official on the report card."

He paused, smiling in his pleasant memory.

"What happened when you showed the report card to your parents?" I asked.

My father's smile faded. "Oh, nothing happened. Nobody noticed it. If they did, nobody said anything."

"Really? So, from that day on you were Billy McCollough?" I asked.

"Yep. Well, until I got a job as a geologist for Alcoa. I had to go to South America for a business trip and needed a passport. My birth certificate read Thompson so they wouldn't give me a passport for McCollough. I panicked. I was afraid I'd lose my job for pretending to be someone I wasn't. But it turned out not to be a big deal. I went to court and they changed it legally."

He stopped to suck on his teeth as though he were trying to remove something wedged between them. He did this all the time, so I knew there was nothing stuck in his teeth. It was his personal punctuation.

"Just think," he went on. "If I hadn't done that, all you kids would've been illegitimate, too!"

I looked up at him, a question on my face. How would we be illegitimate? "Here you had grown up thinking you were McColloughs," he said, and you had really been Thompsons." He laughed his nervous Yogi Bear laugh.

"Tell me what happened when your brother Dick died," I said, wincing even as the words came out of my mouth. Too direct, too quick. I suddenly felt I had created a clinical interviewing practicum for myself, where I was the interviewer as well as the supervisor.

Silence fell between us. My father looked down at the empty cup in his hands, his face softening. As I waited, I realized Dick's name hadn't made that long list of siblings which had tumbled out of family members' mouths in a cadence practiced over many years. Billy, Peggy, Trudy, Judy, Donnie, Donna and Kathy.

"He died of a busted appendix," my father said. "By the time they got him to the hospital, the poison was already all through his system and he died."

I sat quietly, waiting for him to go on.

"He was eleven, I think." He paused as though he were calculating in his head. "I wasn't around at the time. I was in the Merchant Marines up at the Great Lakes."

I felt a knot in my stomach. It seemed I'd known this story my whole life. I didn't remember ever being told it, or by whom—it was as if I'd been born knowing it. I almost couldn't bear to put him through the telling of it. I felt a strong urge to skip ahead to the next period of his life, to fill in the painful space that had suddenly come into the room. Yet something held me there, steady, listening.

"I came home, of course." he said.

Tears came to my eyes as I remembered the part of the story he wasn't going to tell. Nobody in his family even tried to find him to tell him his brother had died. It was a fourteen-year-old girl down the street who'd had a crush on him who found out where he was located and sent him a telegram. It was my mother.

"I always felt guilty about Dick's death. I was the oldest son, and if I hadn't run away, maybe he wouldn't have died."

"Why would he have been your responsibility, Dad? Weren't your parents around?" I asked.

I felt disingenuous with this question. I knew the broad brushstrokes but wanted more detail.

"My mother was in the hospital," he said. "She was always in the hospital for one reason or another. I think she just couldn't cope and would go in and have a breakdown.

So she was in the hospital and Gus was probably drinking and left Peggy in charge, who was probably around ten years old. Dick got real sick and she didn't know what to do. I don't really know all the details because, as I said, I wasn't there."

"Wasn't that around the time Donna was given away?"

I was shocked to hear these words come out of my mouth. So matter of fact, a simple question, with a nonchalance so uncharacteristic of any discussion of this topic it felt as if it were a cold, clinical dissecting knife opening a wound. Because Donna had returned after eighteen years, nobody ever mentioned she'd been gone. And certainly, there was no mention of why or how she went.

My father looked at his cup again. "You know that story, Barb," he said quietly. "You've asked me about it before."

I cringed. He was right, of course. I knew the facts--that Donna, the seventh of eight children, had been adopted out. Although I had asked about it before, perhaps many times before, I had never been given an answer that satisfied me.

"I've only heard bits and pieces over the years," I said. "I'd like to hear the whole thing from your point of view."

He sighed deeply. "Ok, Barb, for you. Geez, what you put your old man through!"

Although he was trying to make light of the moment, I could feel his deep sorrow, the pain he battled so valiantly to keep at bay with his mock jocularity, a deep sludge in the bottom of his heart which from time to time showed itself through his eyes.

"Let's see," he began. "I do think it was after Dick died. My mother was in the hospital again. Maybe she had a little bit of a breakdown after Dick's death. Donna was just a baby then, maybe a year old, and Gus couldn't take care of the whole family. You know, work and take care of a little baby as well as the rest of the kids. So the next-door neighbors, the Alters, took her."

"Dad," I said, impatience rising to the surface. "This is the part of the story I never get. I totally understand the crisis of a death and then your mother's breakdown and neighbors helping out. The part I *don't* get is that they never got her back!"

"You always get so worked up about this. You'd think we'd given *you* away. They officially adopted her, Barb," he said, his voice intensifying . "And then they moved away."

"But didn't they still live in the same town?" I asked. "And didn't they have any connection to her? And then Grandma went on to have Kathi?"

Despite my best efforts, I was getting riled up. None of this made any sense to me. My father had gone quiet, as always happened when this topic came up.

"I'm sorry, Dad. I didn't mean to get carried away. It just has always baffled me. Why don't we take a little bathroom break? Do you want something more to drink?"

While my father was in the bathroom, I went into the kitchen and put the tea kettle on to boil. I knew more about the Donna situation than my father realized, but it was nevertheless still a mystery to me. My father's youngest sister Kathi was one year older than I. I have no memories of her until grade school when, during our annual visits to Pennsylvania, she and I would play together.

One thing we loved to do was make peanut butter toast and cut it up in fancy shapes and serve it to the adults who were sitting around the table talking, smoking and drinking coffee.

As we grew into teenagers, we became especially close. One day, Kathi (who had changed the 'y' to an 'i' in her name) was told by her mother (and my grandmother), "Go get dressed. We're going to your sister's graduation party." Kathi had no idea what her mother was talking about. She got dressed and when they arrived at a party, she met her sister, Donna, for the first time. Kathi immediately recognized her as the girl whose photo was included in Christmas cards from her mother's *friend* Mabel who Kathi had always thought looked just like her. The only thing Kathi remembers from that day is the pocketbook they gave Donna for a present. She was never told anything else, and from that day on, Donna re-entered the family as if she had been there all along.

As I poured my tea, I realized I could stop right here in my interview with my father.

When he returned from the bathroom, I could just start talking about what we were going to do today—and just move on. He'd believe we'd completed our interview.

No. I had to keep going.

As we settled again in the living room, I said, "I really appreciate you doing this, Dad. I know sometimes it's not easy to talk about the past. Are you doing okay with this?"

"Oh sure, Barb. I'm fine," he said, with a quick little clench in his jaw. He leaned forward and took up his water glass.

"Let's go back to where we left off, then," I said. "You mentioned you ran away from home. Tell me about that."

"One day, I was waiting for my friend Kippy Henry to come by so we could walk to school as we did every morning." I felt him relax into the telling of the story, and I relaxed, too.

"Well, don't he show up in his father's big green Buick! He says, 'Come on, get in, my dad gave me the car today.' To tell you the truth, I didn't believe him, because he didn't have his license and it didn't seem like something his father would do. But what the heck. It wasn't my problem. So off we went.

"Kippy was stupid enough to drive close to the school. He just had to show off to the girls, I guess. Mr. Grayson, the Vice Principal, saw us and turned us in. The principal kicked us out and told us we couldn't come back until our fathers came in with us. Gus wouldn't go in with me, so I couldn't go back to school. I was so disgusted I ran away from home and joined the Merchant Marines."

"God, that's incredible! That was the end of school for you just because your father wouldn't come in and vouch for you?"

"That's the way it was back then, Barb. And my dad was a bullheaded guy, especially if he had been drinking."

"So why couldn't your mother go?"

"I don't know. I don't even remember if I asked her. The principal specifically asked for our fathers. Kippy's came and he got back into school." He paused as if to rest on a long walk.

"Life was different back then," he went on. "There were no social workers and counselors and those kinds of people in the schools. The principal was king." He paused and sucked on his teeth. "I hated that guy."

"So, that's when you ran away from home?"

He nodded.

"So, you were in the Merchant Marines. Then you got a telegram from Mom that your brother had died and you came home. Did you go back to the Great Lakes after the funeral?"

"No, I couldn't. I'd had to jump ship trying to get back home. When they caught me, I had to admit I had lied about my age to get into the Merchant Marines, so they had to let me go. That forever burned my bridges with the Merchant Marines," he said.

I was surprised how easily he admitted to lying. Not that I ever thought he was a sterling truthteller. I had seen many examples of white lies, of him reshaping reality for his convenience or to save face in some circumstance. In fact, I had noticed over the years that my father had a relative relationship to the truth, selecting a version of reality the way he would select a shirt for the day. Yet the greatest transgression for which his children would be punished was if they lied. I had never before heard him admit to lying.

I paused, wondering if it would be advantageous to follow this idea of the lie. What tactic would make him most open to telling me the true story of my own birth? His greatest pain, I knew, was not that he was illegitimate, not that he never knew his father. It was that his mother refused to tell him who his father was. This was one issue I would never bring up with him. I knew from my mother that my dad's mother had told him she would reveal his father's identity before she died. I knew my father was holding out hope that she would keep her word. I decided not to go there.

"So, what did you do when you didn't go back to the Merchant Marines?" I asked.

"Oh, I don't know." He paused to suck his teeth once again. "I got a job with Meadow Gold Dairy. Then I went into the Navy."

Silence fell between us. He cleared his throat and again reached for the glass of water next to his chair.

"You know your mother was pregnant when we got married, don't you?"

Just as he began to speak, my mother entered the far end of the living room on her way into the kitchen. For one electric millisecond, my eyes met hers and I saw what seemed like a mixture of fear and rage pass over her face.

I held my breath, as though by doing so I could stave off the betrayal playing out before my eyes. I had never been told this information, but in the moment, I recognized I had known it nonetheless.

But I was stunned by my father's cavalier presentation of this fact. He had to have known it had never been shared with us. How could he have colluded in hiding it for thirty years and then pretend it was common knowledge?

My mind was suddenly like a quick-moving Rolodex, flipping through the past for evidence, both of the secret and the knowing of the secret. The confusion about the day of their anniversary, always missing it by a day, when in fact it was the year that was off by one. I realized on some level, all three of us kids had known, because the idea of creating a celebration for their twenty-fifth wedding anniversary had never arisen.

My mind returned to the present moment, rejoining my father mid-story. My mother had gotten what she wanted from the kitchen and came back into the living room. She paused at my father's chair, listening. I found it painful to watch her, wondering what must be going on inside her, what it must feel like to be so exposed, to be betrayed by your spouse.

My thoughts swam desperately from point to point. I

was horrified that my father had done this, and yet I was grateful he had done this. I felt my mother would never in her entire lifetime release herself from carrying this lie. I wondered if my father had known she was coming into the room just then? Was it really a betrayal if he had consciously done it to free her—to free them both from this extortionate lie?

Glancing at my mother, I interrupted my father. "God, it's so terrible that you had to keep such a secret for all these years. I know in those days it was considered a shameful thing, but now it's not such a big deal."

I stopped, my own words sounding hollow to me, like pennies being pitched across the divide in great earnest, but never hitting the mark. I couldn't bear to feel inside myself what I imagined my mother was feeling. I wanted desperately to say something to soothe her, to soothe myself.

"Joyce doesn't know this," my mother said coolly.

So *that* was the issue, I thought. Shielding Joyce from the knowledge that she'd been conceived out of wedlock.

To protect Joyce? Or to protect herself from Joyce's potential wrath at this discovery?

I sighed. There was something in this moment with my parents which felt strangely familiar, like unbeknownst to anyone present, a gaseous substance had leaked into the room and it was beginning to render each of us mute, our brains becoming foggier by the second, the urge to flee for air rising in increasing desperation per second. I became aware of myself struggling to stay alert, even as my chest tightened as though a band were being cinched bit by bit.

After an uncomfortable silence, my father began to talk again. This time I didn't interrupt him. My mother turned without comment and left the room.

"Your mother got pregnant right around the time Dick died," he said. How bizarre, I thought, as though I were listening to his story from an observation point high above the room. He made it sound as if there was a cause and effect between Dick dying and Mom getting pregnant—somehow having nothing to do with him.

Come to think of it, I had never heard anything about my parents' early days except that she'd sent him a telegram when his brother died. He'd already said he came home for the funeral. Was it then that Joyce was conceived?

"Well, let's see," he went on. "Joyce was born in April, so I guess that means your mother got pregnant around the middle of July."

I coughed to hide the urge to laugh at his charade. They must have counted off those nine months a million times over the years. They were a map so worn with creases there was barely any paper left.

"I kind of panicked," he said. "I didn't know what to do. I didn't have a job. I went off and joined the Navy."

Irritation rose in me. How oblivious could he be? *I joined the Navy*, not *I knocked her up and ran away*.

"So what happened to Mom?" I asked.

"Oh, I think she must have gone back into the bedroom," he said.

His response, though concrete, was evidence to me that on some level he had taken in what had just happened in the room, some sign that he might be reacting internally to the dynamic which had almost knocked me out, that he would rather answer the question concretely in the here-and-now rather than face the real question I was asking him.

"No, Dad, I mean what happened to her when you ran off?"

"She stayed home with her parents, with Grammie and Pappap," he said. "Then I came back in January and we got married, four months before Joyce was born."

My attention shifted from my father's story to my own beating heart. The next big event in the family's history was when, two-and-a-half years later, he came and took his wife and daughter to make their home at Jacksonville Naval Air Station, whereupon my mother immediately became pregnant with me.

I heard the buzz of my father's voice as though I was hearing it from afar, as he talked about early married life, starting with the blizzard on the day of their wedding, about how he'd had the flu. I'd heard all this before, and with the tension mounting in me the closer we came to my entrance onto the scene, I became impatient.

"So, did Mom go with you then?" I knew she hadn't. I was trying to hurry the story along.

"Naw. I wasn't able to take her with me because..."

"Were you there for Joyce's birth?" I interrupted. I knew he hadn't been.

"No, I couldn't be there," he said. "I didn't see her until she was three weeks old."

"So when did you and Mom set up housekeeping for yourselves?" I asked. *August 1948*, I answered in my own mind. The month I was conceived.

"Gosh, that wasn't until Joyce was about two-and-a-half. I got stationed in Jacksonville and your mother and Joyce came with me. I guess that was August of 1948."

I felt a jab of pain in my stomach. After this whole circuitous route, I feared my nerve would now fail me.

"What was it like when you moved to Jacksonville?" I asked.

Oh, for God's sake, I thought. *Why did I ask that question? Now he'll go on about those damn flapjack days.*

"It was tough," he said. "They didn't have housing for us, so we had to rent a little bungalow nearby. It was small and pretty basic. We were poor then, but your mother was good at stretching a dollar for food. I remember once we ate buckwheat flapjacks for a whole week while we waited for payday. To this day, I can't stand the sight of buckwheat flapjacks!"

"Mom was pregnant with me during that time?" I couldn't believe my voice sounded so thin.

"Yeah, I guess she was."

"That must have been quite a time. You two just getting used to living together for the first time and you already have a two-year-old and another baby on the way."

"Yeah, it was quite a time, all right."

I realized he was not going to make this easy for me. Everything I'd asked he'd answered with vague, brief answers. But then again, I realized, I was asking him vague, stalling questions.

"What happened when I was born?"

"What do you mean?" my father asked.

I had been heading the long way around, the labor, going to the hospital, his first sight of me, the first botched diaper change. But when he asked what I meant, I cut right to the heart of the matter.

"That my birth certificate says I am a twin."

"Oh, Barb. There wasn't anything to that. That was just a clerical mistake," he said.

Much to my surprise, I felt my whole body relax. I

hadn't been aware of how much tension I'd been carrying, not just during this interview, but for the entire last year, how anxious I had been about the possibilities before me. I wanted nothing more than to have my daddy take it all away, to say it wasn't so.

Part of me wanted to stop right there. No need to go any further. We had gotten to the bottom of it. But another part of me pressed on.

"But what about that whole story about Mrs. Wechsler, that Mom thought she heard them say Mrs. Wechsler lost her baby but then it turned out she didn't really..."

"Oh, Barb. That was just a mistake. It's what your mother first thought, but it wasn't true. I'm surprised you remember that story after all these years."

I told my father what had happened at The Dinner Party, when Kim mistook me for you, Kaye.

"... she said, the person I looked exactly like was a person named Kaye Wechsler."

As silence fell between us for the second time in my life, I saw tears spill down my father's cheeks. My whole body flooded with anxiety and dread. I was certain he wasn't crying over a clerical error.

After a considerable silence, I asked, "Why are you crying, Dad?"

He stalled for a moment, fiddling with getting his handkerchief out of his pocket.

"It makes me sad that I've passed on to you what I've had to struggle with my whole life--not knowing who my father is."

I was silent, trying to understand what he'd just said to me. If the story of me being a twin was not true, then he hadn't passed *anything* on to me. I knew he wasn't telling me the whole truth about his tears. I had finally come to a wall I was not prepared to scale. I sat quietly while my father composed himself. Eventually he looked up at me expectantly.

I pulled myself back to my interviewer role.

"Thanks, Dad. I think we've done enough for today."

CHAPTER 9

MARCH 19, 1995

I CAN'T BELIEVE I WROTE SO MUCH TO YOU ABOUT MY interview with my father. I don't know what came over me. Once I started, it all just poured out. I had planned to tell you the wonderful things about my family in advance of your meeting them, but I am learning it's hard to compartmentalize the strictly positive memories from the more complicated ones. I wanted to be neutral, to give you an opportunity to meet them and form your own opinions based on your experience.

Truth is, I have been having a conversation with you in my head for at least the last twenty years, if not before. So once I am addressing you directly, I can't hold back!

————

The interview with my father left me unsettled. I didn't know how to interpret his tears or his explanation of them. I knew he didn't mean what his words implied. There could be no doubt that I was my father's daughter--that was not the uncertainty he'd passed on to me. His immediate emotional response to my story about being mistaken for you seemed very strong, if in fact there was no basis for the story at all. And if it had been an innocent switch of which he knew nothing then his response was even harder to fathom. It dawned on me that there was a secret about my birth that my father knew and wouldn't admit, just as his mother would never tell him the secret of his own birth--in his case, who his father was. That was what he must have meant by, "I've passed on to you what I have struggled with my whole life." But what was this secret I felt so sure he knew?

Although I had planned to interview both parents during that summer visit in 1976, it was several years later when I finally did a similar interview with my mother. I don't remember any discussion about postponing my mother's portion of my so-called "project."

After my interview with my father, we all just dropped the topic. Automatic shutdown of the system at the threat of a toxic leak, a drill so practiced in our family none of us even noticed when it had gone into effect.

I realized this morning that I have said very little about my (our?) mother. It is much more difficult for me to try to even capture her essence.

When I think of her as a young girl, two images come to mind. One is from a photograph of her, a tall lanky girl with long, dark, wiry hair. Her slightly-parted lips reveal surprisingly large teeth. It's hard to tell if she is smiling demurely or if she just doesn't have enough lip to go around. She stands stiffly in her band uniform, its light-colored jacket a quiet background for a splash of military braid across the chest and down the sleeves. Although the photo is in black and white, I picture that braid, as well as the buttons down the front and at the wrists, as being bright gold. Her small, square hat hides her dark bush of hair, its large plume rising upward like a fountain. Resting on her left hip and extending outward toward the camera is her glockenspiel and in her right hand is the hammer.

I love this picture of my mother. Although she looks remarkably grown-up and confident for a twelve-year-old, I think of it as evidence that my mother had some happy, confident, optimistic moments in her youth. All the other pictures from my mother's childhood appear depressing to me. Perhaps it's the photographic technology of the day, with all those sepia tones, or maybe, since photography was still a novelty, people self-consciously struck more serious poses. When I see my mother standing erect, side-by-side with her older brother Rich, both of them behind a small bench upon which sits her younger siblings Chuck and Patty, all of their faces are unsmiling. Even as a child, when I looked at those photos, I'd wonder if my mother was sick or sad about something. Truth be told, most pictures of her as an adult have this same sorrowful quality, as well.

But in the photo with the glockenspiel, she looks happy and strong.

I know my mother loved that photo, too. She loved to say the word *glockenspiel* and would giggle with us when we were little and attempted to say it. I think she liked that we had such a big, important-sounding word to learn about her life, just as we had struggled with the word *geologist* for my father. *Glockenspiel*. My mother played the *glockenspiel*. It made me feel smart to know such a word and proud to have a mother who played such a grand instrument.

One time, Aunt Pat came to visit and together we were looking through old photo albums.

"Look, Harriet," she said to my mother. "Here's a picture of you playing the bells in the high-school band."

"No, Aunt Pat," I corrected her. "That's the *glockenspiel*."

I can still feel my mother smile.

The other image I have of my mother as a girl is not a photograph, but rather a collage in my mind, pieced together from bits of her history I've gleaned over the years. It's a hot August afternoon in 1945. My mother is fifteen years old. In my mind's eye, I see her alone on a dusty Western Pennsylvania road wearing a pink gingham sundress, her mat of thick hair tied up to keep her neck cooler in the summer sun. With a serious look on her face, she focuses on picking black raspberries from the roadside bushes. She is fretting about whether there are enough berries left to bake a pie for her sweetheart Bill, and she's nervous about the bees swarming around her.

She has no idea she is three weeks pregnant, no idea that upon hearing this news, Bill will become so scared and ashamed he will run off and join the Navy, leaving her to the wrath of her alcoholic father.

Nor does she know that as she picks her raspberries, a bomb is being dropped on her behalf, a bomb with the destructive capability never before known, that will kill thousands of Japanese civilians and fatally poison countless others, forever changing the world she has known, the world her unborn child will enter.

The history of the world, I believe, is handed down, not only through our minds and through the events we record. It's encoded in our cells and in our consciousness and is passed through placentas into the blood and the bone of the next generation. Our personal histories, our cultural histories, humanity's history. Instantaneous and complete, stored in the human body.

Whether we are aware of it or not, the truth is in the body.

The truths the body holds onto are the ones the mind has lied about, the secret shames to which we can't give voice, the losses we are not supposed to know about, the feelings that don't match our desired version of reality. The soul knows who and what it is and will defend its integrity in the body at all costs. The body will distort itself, disease itself, even kill itself before it will incorporate a falsehood. The body has tremendous storage capacity, but eventually it goes on a rampage, attempting to clean itself out through illness, madness or mishap.

By the time I was four, I would compulsively wring my hands, but this gesture was insufficient to dispel my distress, and I soon developed incapacitating headaches and stomachaches. In its simple wisdom, my body had switched to symptoms that were impossible to ignore and certainly beyond the reach of disciplinary action. I was admitted to Children's Hospital in Pittsburgh for suspected ulcers and migraines.

My mother dressed me in my best dress and patent leather shoes.

"Birthday party?" I asked.

"No, honey. We're going to Pittsburgh," She said this with considerable enthusiasm.

"The zoo!" I exclaimed, naming the only destination I knew called *Pittsburgh*.

My mother laughed. "We're going to see a doctor who will take your stomachaches away."

After a very long drive, we arrived at a gigantic building.

Once inside, we met a lady who bent down close to my face and asked, "How are you, Barbara?"

"Finethankyouandyou?" I replied. I didn't understand why the lady laughed. This was what my daddy had taught me to say when someone asked how I was. It wasn't supposed to be a joke.

The lady took me into a small room and took off my party dress and shoes. Then she took me by the hand and we went into a room where there were lots of children in cages. It was just like the zoo, except there were children instead of animals. Some of them were screaming and shaking the bars, some were silently crying and others just stared at us as we walked to the far side of the room where the lady put me into one of the empty cages.

I stayed in that cage for a very long time, although my parents insist it was only a week. They said they came to visit me as often as they were allowed. I believe them--I just don't remember. My father tried to explain that I wasn't in a cage--it was a crib with a top on it to keep us from climbing out. The only visitor I remember is the juice lady, who was very nice and came once a day and gave us delicious things to drink. Other than that, the only visitor was the man who came and put me on his rolling table to go far away to a place where they gave me nasty-tasting milk and made me lie on a cold table while a big machine took pictures of my head and my belly. Nothing they did to me actually hurt, but I was scared the whole time I was there.

Finally my mother came and took me home. She was very happy because the doctor had told her I wasn't sick. I was just a nervous kid, or as my parents described me, a *worrywart*. I was happy to see my mother and get out of the hospital, but I didn't understand what was going to make the stomachaches stop.

Soon after the good news that I was just a worrywart, my mother took me to J.C. Penney's to have a Pixie Pin-Up made. In the sepia photograph, I am posed in a perky posture, one foot up on the table beside me, elbow on knee, fleshy little hand scrunched up against a squishy cheek. An enormous pin-wheel bow that matches my pinafore hovers above each ear, holding back wispy curls. On my face is a Shirley Temple smile. I see that picture and my stomach hurts. I search her face for clues of distress. The one possibility is in the far-off look in her eye.

'How are you, Barbara?'

'Finethankyouandyou?'

CHAPTER 10

FALL 1976

WE ALL PACKED UP, LITERALLY AND FIGURATIVELY, AFTER the interview with my father in the summer of 1976. My parents returned to Virginia, and I headed west to Chicago for my second internship.

————

I was not happy that Smith, even though I had again requested a small social service agency on the East Coast, assigned me to the Psychiatric and Psychosomatic Institute, an outpatient facility within a large urban hospital on the south side of Chicago. I had never travelled to the Midwest, and everything about it seemed foreign to me: the intensity and impersonality of life in a large sprawling city, the busyness and bustle this Virginia girl experienced as unfriendliness.

Then again, stress, sadness and loss clouded the eye of this beholder. Once again, as in Boston the year before, I knew no one, so I slept on the couch of a friend of a friend of a friend. This made me desperate to have a bed and a room of my own.

Unlike the ease with which I'd found a roommate in Boston, finding that bed and room became a Sisyphean task. Unlike that first big move to Boston, I didn't have the energy to tackle something new. In fact, painfully cut off from anything familiar, I felt bereft. Even though Nick called me every single morning when he got to work, exuding support and comfort, it was as if it dribbled out of the receiver onto my ear and then to the floor. Nothing penetrated the armor I had constructed around myself. Nick, although nice, lived fifteen-hundred miles away.

I was alone.

When I reported to my internship, the huge, impersonal, antiseptic environment dismayed me. Although my supervisor officially welcomed me, her formality and distance made me wary of her. On the way to my third day at the clinic, as I edged my way through the rush hour traffic in the Loop, I drove over a large metal slab covering an excavation made by the gas company for repairs. Although thousands of cars had passed over that spot before me that morning, when my little butterscotch Toyota crossed over, it shifted and I felt my car sink into the ground. For one horrifying second, as I felt the car sink but before it came to a stop, I felt literally swallowed up by this new city, as if some monster lurking beneath the street had reached up and grabbed me.

A stream of faces gaped in horror as they passed in cars and on foot before the crane came to free me. The tow truck the police called couldn't budge it, and the driver feared further attempts might dislodge the metal plate from its precarious perch and plunge my car, with me in it, further into the hole. I was terrified.

While waiting for the crane, the policemen stood next to my window, joking, in an apparent attempt to either distract or calm me.

"Hey, lady, what are you trying to do, break our streets?"

One policeman pointed to the back seat of my little Corolla. "Yeah, ya got so much stuff in there, you must've broken the road."

The other policeman, looking at the pillows, lamps and books in the back seat, chimed in. "Say, where are you going with all that stuff? Are you running away from home or something?"

I tried to muster a laugh, knowing they were doing their best to cheer me up, but instead tears crowded into my eyes.

"No, I just arrived here a couple of days ago to work at Michael Reese. I'm sleeping on a friend's sofa. I don't even have a place to live yet!" I heard the desperation in my shrill voice.

"Hey, in that case, Bob, I think we should arrest her for vagrancy."

They were doing their best to make me laugh.

At that point, a man emerged out of the crowd of tourists standing at the curb of The Palmer House. He held up his camera and offered to take a photo before the car was removed in case I needed it for the insurance.

"Thank you," I said. "That's a good idea."

"Yes," he said, "I'm returning to Austria today, but I'll get the film developed and send the photo to you right away."

He took several snaps of me posing with the policemen.

"Okay, so now if you will give me your address so I can send them to you..."

The reminder that I didn't have a home brought tears to my eyes once again. He looked at me with a puzzled expression. One of the policemen stepped in and gave him the address of Michael Reese, then turned to me and said, "Just give him your name and the department."

I arrived two hours late to the clinic and I told my supervisor what had happened.

"What time did you get to work?" she asked.

God, I thought. *This woman is a robot.*

Years later, when I experienced Star Trek's character Data for the first time, this moment sprang to mind. I was certain they must have fashioned the *pre-emotion chip* Data after my supervisor. And she was the one, who, above anyone I'd met in Chicago, was actually paid to help me adjust. The despair I felt in that moment was more distressing to me than falling into the hole. At least the policemen were kind. At least the passersby showed some degree of interest in my plight.

No, not Toni. It was only, "What time did you get to work?"

After several weeks, I found a comfortable, affordable place to live right in Lincoln Park with Nina, an alum from Smith. Although this broke the horror of those first weeks, I never felt at home in Chicago, never lost that deep feeling of anxiety and isolation—no matter how many friends I made, no matter how involved I became in my work.

It wasn't until I had been in Chicago for more than six months that I was able to understand why I felt so anxious and alone.

In 1966, ten years before I moved to Chicago, at the

end of my sophomore year in high school, my sister Joyce, then a freshman in college, became pregnant. I learned of this one night when I came home from a sock hop at the school. The living room was dark when I came in and, I assumed, empty, until I saw the glow of a cigarette. My mother was sitting in the rocking chair, and as my eyes adjusted to the dark, I saw that my father was sitting on the couch.

"What's wrong?" I asked, fearing they were lying in wait for me, ready to punish me for some transgression I didn't yet know about.

"Come on in, Barb" my father said. "We have something we want to talk to you about."

My mother was strangely silent, smoking her cigarette. I sat down on the footstool near her chair.

"Joyce is going to have a baby," my father said.

Oh my God, I thought. *This will kill my mother.*

On pure instinct, I left the footstool and sat at her feet, not knowing why I thought she was endangered, but knowing I needed to be close enough to contain her if she exploded or self-immolated. Even stranger was that I imagined that I could.

"When?" I asked, still not believing what I'd heard.

My mother mumbled a response.

"Tomorrow?!" I asked, incredulous.

"March," my mother mumbled again, irritation in her voice, as my father chuckled at my absurd question.

I was so preoccupied with the certainty that this was going to kill my mother, I don't remember all the details they told me that night. I had no idea why I felt my mother was so vulnerable. I would have thought I'd be fearing for Joyce's safety from my mother's wrath. They told me Joyce was asleep in their room. I didn't understand why she wouldn't be in her own bed, in the room she and I shared.

The next few months were a haze to me. I remember overhearing fighting between my mother and Joyce.

"How could you let him fuck you without protection?" I was shocked. I

didn't know my mother even knew this word. It was ugly coming from her mouth.

"Why not? You did!"

Another shock to me. How would Joyce know this, I wondered.

I heard the unmistakably crisp sound of palm against cheek, then the clatter of feet, followed by the slam of a door.

The next five months had been pretty grim around our house. None of us had any friends visit. We never talked about what was happening. We just silently went about our business, acting as if everything was normal.

In January, Joyce left for the Florence Crittendom Home in Georgetown, where she lived until she gave birth to a little girl in March, whom she named Colleen before giving her up for adoption.

I had known the plan all along, as did my maternal grandmother. Otherwise, it was a closely guarded secret, even from my eleven-year-old brother Billy. I never understood my parents' decision not to tell him, as he was a bright, precocious boy. Surely he would notice that his sister had grown a very big belly and if he did, he would know what that meant.

On the day Joyce left for the Crittendom Home she left behind a letter for Billy saying she had a sudden, exciting three-month job opportunity in Chicago, and she had to leave right away. This story was also given to the extended family back in Pennsylvania.

That afternoon, when I got off the school bus, I saw Billy coming to meet me. He was looking dejectedly at his feet, kicking some piece of debris as he made his way down the hill. When he got to me, he lifted his sad eyes to mine and simply said, "She's gone."

I didn't say anything at first. I had been expecting him to come running to tell me the news. "Guess what? Joyce got a chance to go to Chicago for a job!" Something to that effect. I didn't know what to say to his reaction. We walked home in silence.

It wasn't until years later, after I'd finished graduate school and understood more about family dynamics, that I remembered that scene. I realized how painfully isolated Billy must have been, how clear it was that he knew what was going on but was not permitted to acknowledge that he knew. One day, as he and I were driving along in my car, I decided to bring it up.

"You know Bill, I was thinking about the time Joyce was pregnant, and she went away to have a baby..."

He looked at me blankly. "What are you talking about?" he asked.

"You know, when you were about eleven, Joyce got pregnant, and..."

As I filled in the story he continued to stare at me. He didn't believe me. He'd had no awareness of it, no memory whatsoever.

"Wow," he said after a while. "I've never been able to figure out why, with my excellent memory, I've never been able to remember a single thing about my eleventh year. I can't remember the teacher I had, the friends I played with-

-nothing. It's like a blank screen on my tape. This really blows me away."

So for me, on an unconscious level, being in Chicago was being in the place of banishment, of exile from the family hearth. During the months Joyce was "in Chicago," nobody ever asked for her address or telephone number to be in touch with her. Nobody ever, in all the years since, asked Joyce about Chicago or her "work" there. We had all so successfully repressed the event that even when I was assigned to Chicago, I never made the connection. I never questioned the dread I felt in my stomach at the prospect of going there. And yet it seems nonetheless, going to Chicago meant falling into the void, the place where no one would find me, the place associated, somewhere in my psyche, with a forfeited child, a member of the family never known.

While I was in Chicago, I had a memorable dream. I dreamed I was in a living room with my entire extended family when a male visitor arrived. He sat on a chair opposite the couch on which I sat with my mother and other family members. I was the only one to interact with the visitor, while the family stood mutely encircling the room, watching. All the while I was speaking, my mother was pulling at my face, yanking my mouth and eyes into distorted shapes. I continued to interact with the stranger, pretending nothing was going on. None of the relatives showed concern, and the visitor didn't seem to notice what was happening to me. Suddenly, my mother thrust two fingers up my nose. In pain, I automatically reacted by biting down on her hand. With this, the entire room full of relatives turned on me in horror and said, "How could you do that to your mother?" I got up and frantically searched for a phone to call my cousin Rick to come and get me. When I found a phone, its numbers were all scrambled, making it impossible to dial. I awoke from this dream sobbing, with mucous streaming from my nose.

I was shaken to the core by this dream. For days it replayed in my mind, as though it was an event that had actually happened, and I found myself defending myself to myself for hurting my mother.

"It was reflex!" I mentally argued to that roomful of relatives. "She was hurting *me*!" And why was I the spokesperson for the whole family? A chill came over me when I associated the demeanor of the man in the dream with a Child Protective Service worker I had met who had gone to investigate a report of child abuse, and the child in question was in the room as the adults denied there was any problem. The case was closed.

The feeling of that dream lasted for weeks and it surprises me even now, twenty-years later, that it still makes my stomach churn and my face sting as I tell it to you, Kaye.

CHAPTER 11

SPRING 1977

I EASILY SETTLED INTO THE APARTMENT WITH NINA NEAR the Lincoln Park Zoo and we quickly became good friends. One day she told me she questioned her sexuality but felt too timid to go anywhere alone to places where she might meet a potential partner. A new lesbian-owned restaurant had recently opened on the Northside and she invited me to go there for dinner so she could check it out.

"Of course!" I said.

I had a number of gay friends, both men and women. Two of the six bridesmaids in my wedding were lesbians, and my cousin Rick, with whom I was very close, had come out a few years before. He'd moved from Pennsylvania to D.C for a job as a computer programmer and had lived with my parents. He'd been an effeminate young boy and there were many clues throughout his life that he would grow up to be gay. One day, my mother called me in my apartment in Alexandria, telling me she thought Rick was using drugs. She described how he had been coming home later and later and then had started staying away over-night. When he did call and she tried to question him about his whereabouts or activities, all he would say is, "I love it, I love it!"

As my mother went on about her certainty that Rick was now either crazy or a drug addict, I immediately realized what was happening--Rick was coming out at last. I phoned him.

"Rick, I just talked to my mom and she's worried about you," I said.

"Oh no, everything is fine. In fact, it's *great*," he answered. I could see why Mom thought he was on drugs. For a moment, I wondered if my assumption was wrong.

"Rick, I don't mean to pry, but I get a sense you might have a new relationship."

"Oh, I love it, I love it..."

"My mom thinks you are on drugs or going crazy. You need to tell her the truth," I said.

The next time I visited my mother, she tearfully told me she'd learned what was wrong with Rick. He was gay. Through copious tears, she enumerated all the things that were wrong with being gay, all the things which upset her when she thought about having a gay nephew.

As she blew her nose and wiped her eyes, she turned and looked me right in the eye as she asked, "Have you ever...?"

"No, Mom," I could honestly say. "I have never been in a gay relationship."

She calmed. "Well, if you ever do, I don't want to know about it!"

———

Nina and I entered the large, sparsely-furnished rectangular room which had become Mama Peaches restaurant. The smell of varnish from the high-gloss wood floors gave away the age of the establishment. There was a buzz of excitement in the air which translated into the overly-friendly greetings of the hostess and the waitstaff.

"This is cool," Nina said, looking around the room at the other diners before opening her menu. I ordered the vegetarian lasagna and Nina ordered a basil-pesto pasta dish. I found the lasagna delicious, the best I'd ever eaten. I am not sure Nina even tasted her pasta dish, she was so engaged with her surroundings and with talking to various staff.

We walked back to Sedgwick Street in the crisp evening.

"I'm going to work there part-time," she said.

"Really?"

I was stunned. Nina was a well-established professional family therapist. I couldn't imagine her doing waitressing on the side.

"Yeah, just a couple of nights a week," she said. "It would be a good way to meet people in the women's community. And a little extra cash never hurts."

In the weeks ahead, Nina came to know the other staff and started going out for drinks after work. One night she called just as I was about to get dressed for bed.

"Hey, we're going to Petunia's. Why don't you come and meet us?"

I hesitated.

"Come on," Nina said. "It's Friday night! Why sit home alone?"

When I arrived at the bar, everyone from the restaurant was getting up to dance. Nina greeted me quickly and as she turned to join the others, she said, "It's great you're here. Will you save the table for us?"

I sat at the table watching the group dance.

I came out on a cold night for *this?*

Bored, I wondered what was on TV that I might be missing. I broke out of my reverie when a tall woman with black hair and equally black eyes approached the table.

Oh no. I hoped she wasn't going to ask me to dance.

She didn't. Without so much as a glance in my direction, she simply sat down at the other side of the table, watching the group on the dance floor.

Oh-oh. I'd been given the simple job of saving the table. I figured I'd better do something.

"Excuse me, but this table is taken," I said.

She tilted her head back at an angle so it appeared as if she were looking down at me. She just studied me for a moment with a smirk on her face and a little gleam in her eye. "Isn't this where the people from Mama Peaches are sitting?"

"Y-yes!" I stammered, a little too enthusiastically. "Do you work there?"

"I'm an owner," she said cooly, immediately dismissing me by returning her gaze to the dance floor.

I bit my lip, checking my impulse to blurt out, "You must be Mama Peaches!" I didn't know how to act with this intense chick, but I had a feeling *sweet little Virginia girl* wasn't going to win me many points.

I sat silently, trying to look natural, relaxed even, as though I came to these places all the time. I didn't know how to act without chit-chat, and this lady was no chitter or chatter. I found myself wanting her to interact with me and yet felt terror at the thought that she would turn and look at me or ask me a question.

———

The next morning, I was awakened by the ring of the telephone. I picked up reflexively as I had done at this time for the last eight months.

"Hello?" I said, becoming more alert as the seconds passed.

"You're not alone," Nick said. I looked to my left and realized he was right, I *wasn't* alone. How could he tell? Just by my voice?

"Who is he?" Nick demanded.

"It's not a he," I said, shocking myself that it was true, and also that I had stated it so matter-of-factly.

Silence.

Then more silence.

"I don't know what to say," he said.

"Let's talk later," I said.

I hung up and lay back. Fortunately, the phone had not awakened Janet. I studied her face. Seeing her with her eyes closed felt as if I was sneaking something, watching her without her knowledge. Her straight dark hair spread across her cheek. The smell in the air was more restaurant than sex. Without opening her eyes, the inert head spoke.

"I don't know who was on the other end of that call, but it was somebody who is really tuned into you."

I didn't answer. What in the hell have I done? I had never cheated on Nick, and I had never slept with a woman. And here I had done both in one fell swoop.

I don't remember exactly how I managed to bring her home with me that night. It was a behavior I had not engaged in with anyone since moving to Chicago eight months earlier, much less a woman. Much less, EVER on the first night of meeting someone. I could blame alcohol consumption, but I'd never been a big drinker. Then again, maybe I'd had more than usual because of the awkward circumstances I'd been in.

It had surprised me when Nick called, but why should it surprise me when he called every morning? The fact that he knew something was up just from my *hello* told me he was more aware of me than I was of myself.

———

By the time we talked later, Nick had spent more time pondering what this development meant than I had. He was grief-stricken.

"I honestly don't know how to respond," he said. "If you were with another man, I could mount a plan to get you back. I could fly out there to be with you. But how can I compete with a woman?"

I was numb. On one hand, I was touched that he was so tuned in to me and I was also surprised that he would take this development so seriously. He didn't engage in petulance. He didn't trivialize same-sex relations. He took it deep into himself and instantly moved into grief.

I didn't know how to categorize this event, which had all the markings, not of a one-night stand, but of a new relationship. I had never been interested in women before and I didn't know where this would lead. Probably not far, at least not with Janet, for a number of reasons. We couldn't have been more different. She was a very tough white woman who'd grown up in a chaotic home on the South Side of Chicago. From the time she was an adolescent, she'd slept with her clothes on so she would be ready to act quickly in the event of violence, whether in her home or on the streets. I liked her and respected her, but I knew there was too much of a gap in our respective histories. We could never fit into each other's lives.

The only photo I have of the two of us is walking side by side. I was wearing a spring-green polyester dress beneath a traditional beige London Fog trench coat. All that was missing to complete the look were white gloves and a pillbox hat. She was dressed in well-worn soiled jeans and a ripped T-shirt. She was on her way to help start a women's militia.

The visual of our styles spoke as much to our mismatch as did our activities--she, the enraged one ready to incite women to take to the streets, I, the soft-spoken, conservative social worker who just wanted to help people find themselves.

I had no idea that first I'd have to find myself.

CHAPTER 12

MARCH 20, 1995

KAYE!

This process is driving me crazy. It has been seven days since I sent the letter to you. My rational mind knows that's not long at all, but it feels like an eternity. My mind is starting to make up reasons why you might not respond.

Oh my God! Of course. I just came out to you as I told you the story of my coming out in Chicago and now I am afraid that you will reject me. I have to be realistic. You just might. You may have lived a life which has instilled certain beliefs that a same-sex relationship is wrong. The possibility of that sends a sharp pain to my gut.

It only occurred to me much later that the way I entered into my first relationship with a woman could be connected to my search for you. I didn't put it together that I was sad and lonely and isolated in Chicago, not only because of the city's resonance in my family's psyche, but also because the last contact I'd had with my family before going to Chicago was that interview with my father when he'd cried upon learning about me being mistaken for you. His tears had thrust me into a deep, lonely well inside my body and soul

I'd been dangling over since The Dinner Party nine months prior, a place of longing I did not understand, a cold, empty place which had never been warmed in my relationships with men.

At the time, I assumed I hadn't met the right man. Something about meeting Janet that night opened the possibility that this longing in me could be met in a different way, that the aloof, disconnected part of me would find itself in this aloof, disconnected other.

Ever since that first fling in Chicago, all my relationships have been with women, each bringing a successively deeper connection to myself, and ironically, to you. However, the transition has never been an easy one.

———

I hung up the telephone and just sat, staring out the window.

"What's the matter?" my partner Sally asked.

I turned to look at her.

"My parents are moving to Boston," I said.

"What?" Sally asked, arrested in her trek from the living room to the kitchen. She stood there silently awaiting an explanation. When I didn't respond, she came and sat down beside me.

Sally and I had been happily living together in Cambridge for two years. When I returned to Boston from Chicago, it was immediately clear I wasn't returning to my heterosexual life. Nick had been right to be so distraught-- our relationship could never be the same.

I had gotten a job covering the Neonatal Intensive Care Unit and the Infant and Toddler Medical Unit at Children's Hospital. I loved my work with the families whose children were hospitalized on these divisions.

I'd known Sally for years. She had been the partner of one of my bridesmaids when I'd married my high school sweetheart Frank in 1971 after he'd returned from Vietnam. Kristen had immediately emigrated to Australia after my wedding, and a few years later she returned with her lover Sally, a surprise to us all, because until then, none of us had any idea Kristen was gay. The whole scene was straight out of Mary McCarthy's *The Group* when Lakey returns from Europe with a lesbian lover and upends the world she'd known with her college friends.

Sally and Kristen lived happily in Philadelphia for several years, and it was through them, on my frequent weekend visits from D.C., that I became acquainted with, and genuinely enjoyed, the gay community scene there.

Time moved us all forward in our lives. I broke up with Frank and went to graduate school in Massachusetts. Sometime after that, Sally and Kristen broke up and I'd lost touch with both of them.

When Sally heard through the grapevine that I had come out, she contacted me in Chicago to offer support, which we later joked was to put in her application to get closer to me once she realized it was a possibility to be more than friends. When we had become more than friends, she moved to Boston from Philadelphia to live with me.

Since returning to Boston, I'd had an easy, cordial relationship with my parents, who still lived in Virginia. I saw them once or twice a year and otherwise kept in monthly touch by phone and mail. It was a shock to learn of my father's transfer to Hanscom Air Force Base just outside of Boston for his work with the Defense Department. It was a mere coincidence that would bring them right to my door.

On one hand, I thought it might be nice to have them nearby. We could replicate my grandmother's tradition of Sunday dinners together, yet it was a half hour's drive from Cambridge, which would allow me plenty of space.

But what about them visiting our apartment? I had yet to come out to them. They knew I lived with Sally but assumed it was as roommates, even though they'd known Sally from the old days as Kristen's partner. I didn't want to make it explicit because my mother had in fact instructed me that if had a relationship with another woman, she didn't want to know about it.

Yet here it was, almost ten years later. Did my mother still feel that way? Would she even remember she'd said that? I couldn't figure a way to test the waters.

I asked Sally, "What are we going to do?"

"What can you do? She's made it clear she doesn't want to know. Geez, if she wanted to know, it would be as easy as putting two and two together, but your mother always manages to come up with anything but four."

Once my parents actually arrived in Massachusetts, it wasn't easy to keep my relationship with Sally a secret. It wasn't difficult when Sally and I visited their house. They knew her and welcomed her. In the beginning, it was easy to invite them to our house, as well, because we could easily "de-gay" the place, mess up the guest room, and throw Sally's clothes in another closet.

The problem occurred when they dropped in unexpectedly. It was hard to be relaxed and open in welcoming them with my eyes darting around the room to make sure there were no tell-tale signs. After a time, I realized my mother was suffering with the move to Massachusetts. She was lonely, and it was reasonable for her to have believed she would have a daughter to help her and to hang out with. Although she hadn't expressed it, I knew she felt my efforts to keep her at arms' length were a sign that I didn't love her. She couldn't know that I was trying to protect her from knowing who I was.

———

The following Sunday afternoon, I put my collection of books about having a gay child in a big brown paper bag and drove to my parents' house alone.

My mother greeted me at the door. "Hey! Where's Sally?"

"She had to work this morning," I lied.

"Oh, too bad," she said. "Here let me help you...what's in the bag?"

We made our way into the kitchen and I asked, "Where's Dad?"

"I think he's watching a game," she said.

"There is something I'd like to talk to both of you about," I said. "Could we sit down and have a cup of tea together?"

"Hey, Bill," she yelled down the hall. "Barb's here and she wants you to come out."

My mother busied herself making tea and putting out cups. My father emerged from the TV room.

"Hey, Barb! Good to see you. What's so important it can't wait 'til half-time?"

"Now, Bill...." my mother said, "You're always in front of that TV...."

We sat down at the small round butcher-block table in the kitchen. My father planted himself directly across the table from me and my mother took the chair to my right. They both looked at me expectantly.

My heart felt as if it were beating right out of my chest. I was sure they could see it.

"There's something I want to talk to you about," I began.

Immediately, my father, who was out of my mother's line of sight, began shaking his head.

I paused. What was happening? I furrowed my brow for a second to re-focus and make sure I was seeing correctly. Yes, he was definitely shaking his head at me.

"It's something..." I began again, looking at my mother's now-frozen face, "I--I think you already..."

"Maybe it's something we don't want to know," my father interrupted.

I stopped, at a loss for words. Suddenly my mother burst into tears.

"If you are going to tell us you are gay, I don't condone it, I don't approve of it and I had no idea!" she declared.

My face stung as though my mother had slapped me with her words.

My first response was to deny it and say, "No, I want to tell you I'm having a root canal on Wednesday"... but I knew this was no time to joke or use the ready sarcasm that characteristically masked my anger.

My father put his arm around my crying mother's shoulders, trying to soothe her.

"What is actually upsetting you so much? Is it about having grandkids? Maybe she wouldn't have had kids anyway..." Suddenly I was a third-person, faceless bystander observing a scene.

After a number of minutes watching my father console

my mother, my own gut had become a block of frozen rage. I stood up from the table with a sensation of tearing apart the two sides of Velcro. Suddenly I felt enormous, towering over them.

My mother wasn't soothed, nor would she ever be, not as long as she had one more wound in her arsenal which she could pin on me.

"I am going now," I said, and as I exited the kitchen, on impulse, I took back the bag of books I'd brought to ease their pain.

CHAPTER 13

MARCH 21, 1995

I AWOKE LAST NIGHT WITH A START, BELIEVING SOMEONE HAD broken into the house and hovered nearby. I have these kinds of experiences all the time and even more so now as I am waiting to hear from you.

By now you've probably gotten the sense that my life as a worrywart hasn't changed much over the years, although I've developed more professional language to account for my lifelong diffuse anxiety.

When I got out of the hospital at age four, the doctors didn't have an answer for my stomachaches and headaches. The diagnosis of worrywart, which was more of a personality description, didn't include any plan to relieve my physical or mental suffering. We all just had to get used to me being a scared little girl. I developed ways to hide my fears even from myself, believing that being happy was as simple as putting on a sweet smile.

Then when I was eight-years-old, an incident happened in which I proved, at least to myself, there really were things to be worried about.

———

My father completed his master's degree in geology and accepted a position with Alcoa in Spartanburg, South Carolina. Until that time, we had lived in Western Pennsylvania, always in close range to my grandparents and to my cousins. South Carolina was the first evidence I had that there was life outside of that small universe.

We stayed at a big fancy hotel right in downtown Spartanburg for several weeks after arriving while my parents found housing and enrolled us in school. We had two rooms--one on the third floor for Joyce and me and the other on the fifth floor where my parents and my younger brother Bill lived. In a way, it was exciting, because our room had a double bed and I got to sleep with my sister. It also had a claw-footed tub, which I had never seen before.

I was nervous, not only at being in a new universe, but my parents were seemingly a galaxy away! My parents explained to me that this arrangement was the best the hotel could do to accommodate us.

After Joyce and I had been sealed into the room for the night with strict instructions not to open the door to anyone, I lay awake waiting for the knock from those who would try to intrude upon us. Just who was it my parents worried about coming to our door? I thought about the dark-haired busboy from lunch who had failed to clean the table properly and my father had complained and got him into trouble. He had become annoyed when confronted by his supervisor and I had heard him muttering to himself, probably plotting some revenge on us.

Gee, I thought. *The people who work at the hotel could probably get keys to the rooms if they wanted, so we wouldn't have to worry about a knock. They could just put the key in the lock and come on in while we were sleeping!*

"Joyce! Wake up," I called, knowing that being three years wiser than I, she would know what to do.

"Wha... wha... what's the matter?" she grumbled.

"I'm scared," I said. I told her my theory about the staff being able to get keys and come in while we slept.

"Barb, you're being silly. That's the reason the little gold chain is on the door. When it's latched, nobody can come in, because that little gold chain will stop them."

Joyce was so smart. I felt better.

"So go to sleep," she said.

"Okay. Goodnight," I said.

I lay there in the moonlight watching the little gold chain. I remembered Mom demonstrating how it worked and how to latch it so we'd be safe. I sighed with relief and closed my eyes. Minutes later, I was shaking Joyce awake again.

"Joyce, I'm scared."

"What now?" she snapped.

"I was just thinking..."

"Stop thinking and go to sleep!" She was really mad now.

I couldn't help myself.

"Joyce, listen. What if someone could reach around after they unlocked the door with the key and unlatch the little gold chain?"

"Are you stupid? Why would they bother putting a chain on for protection if someone could reach in and take it off?" she snarled sleepily.

"Well, maybe you're right," I said. "But how do we know for sure?"

With an exaggerated sigh, Joyce threw off the bedcovers and got out of bed.

"Okay, I'll prove it to you!" she said.

"No, *no*! Joyce! We're not allowed to open the door," I cried in terror.

She paid no attention.

"Okay, Barb," she said to me from out in the hall. "Shut the door and put the chain on."

I did as I was told and then waited.

After a few seconds Joyce knocked. "Open the door, Barb," she hissed. "I can't try the chain if the door isn't open!"

I opened the door.

Joyce reached around and with one easy swoop of her hand she unhooked the gold chain and walked into the room. She looked stunned herself at what she had just done.

"*No*," I exclaimed in horror. "Let me try."

I went out into the hall and Joyce latched the chain. I rammed my chubby little arm into the opening. No matter how hard I tried, I couldn't get the chain unlatched. Unfortunately, nor could I get my arm out of the door.

"Joyce, I'm stuck," I said, panic starting to rise in my throat.

After a brief attempt to dislodge my forearm, Joyce called my parents. They called the hotel staff. Within a half-hour I was back in bed nursing a sore arm, upset after a scolding for causing so much trouble, but secure in the knowledge that not everyone could break into our room. We were at least safe from little girls with chubby arms.

———

I wish I could say I outgrew my worrywart nature after that, but in many ways, my fears grew as I did. When I was ten, my father was transferred to Kingston, Jamaica. It was baffling to me how we were going to live on that tiny pink island my father showed us on the atlas.

When we arrived at the Kingston airport, Mrs. Bennett, my father's boss's wife, met us at the airport. My first question to her when she took my hand was, "Is Russia still our enemy here?" When she said yes, my whole body silently convulsed with the shattering of my hope that there could be a place in the world where we could be safe. I was so disappointed that I would still have to walk around in fear.

———

I haven't thought of these incidents for a long time, Kaye. It's interesting that they come up now. Writing you, opening this whole question feels similar. Familiar. Despite being repeatedly told it's just a clerical error, that there is nothing here to be worried about, I've persisted.

Someone is going to be really mad when I find you.

But I'm still excited about that. In fact, the further we go, the more nervous and excited I become.

I came up with something very special for you and I to do together to celebrate our reunion. You probably wouldn't know about this, but every year there is a huge Twins Festival in Twinsburg, Ohio, not too far from Cleveland. Sets of twins come from all over the world to take part. They have a parade and lots of activities. The restaurants and hotels have two-for-one specials and scientists come from all over too, with research protocols, hoping to entice twins to participate. It happens the first full weekend in August.

That gives us a good four months to make plans if we want to go this year.

So, I better get on with my project of writing you the story before we meet. If I remember correctly, I was starting to talk about our mother when I veered off in another direction. I do that a lot. Do you do that, too?

CHAPTER 14

OCTOBER 1979

IT WAS A CLEAR SUNDAY MORNING IN OCTOBER, A YEAR (which seemed like a lifetime) after the Sunday morning when I came out to my parents. It was not altogether surprising that after a brief period of silence, we all picked up as if nothing was unusual. Sally was woven into our lives as if she'd always been there. I continued my work at Children's Hospital, and more Sundays than not, Sally and I were at my parents' house for Sunday dinner.

But on this Sunday, Sally was away and I had dinner with my parents alone. Afterward, I sat with my mother as she hemmed a pair of gray gabardine slacks for my father. I watched those familiar, always moving fingers in a meditative fashion. A soft, pink padded belly of her ring finger pushed against the back end of the needle until it broke the surface of the fabric. Almost simultaneously, her thumb and index finger greeted the needle tip coming up through the other side. Each stitch was a birth of sorts.

All of my mother's love was expressed through her hands, not in a direct caress but through constant work--

sewing, baking, cleaning. Delicate hands with ivory backs and pink palms smelled of onions and Clorox, which was to me the hearty, nourishing fragrances of motherly care.

My mother created magic through those hands. In my junior year in high school, she made me a dress for the prom. The night before the dance, I tried it on and to our dismay, it looked terrible on me. I went to bed distraught about having to look ugly at the dance. When I awoke the next morning, there was a totally new dress, new style and new fabric. It was perfect. She had to have stayed up all night to finish it.

Pleasant memories of my mother's care played in my mind as I watched her hem my father's slacks and I realized for the first time, her expressions of love came, not from hugs and kisses (for which I'd always yearned), but through the needle and thread. As I began to muse about the bolts of fabric, the miles of thread with which she'd loved all of us through a lifetime, her voice broke the silence.

"So, how's the job? Do you like working with kids?" she asked.

"I don't actually work with kids very often," I said. "My job is to interview the parents of infants and toddlers to get a sense of what is going on in general in that child's life that could be contributing to the reason the child is in the hospital."

My mother didn't say anything, so I went on.

"You know, the kids are so young they can't really talk about what's going on with them. They might be responding to changes in the family, such as a divorce, or the death of a grandparent or even of their hamster."

My mother laughed. "Yeah, that would be you! Remember when you were in Children's Hospital? You were a real worrywart. You used to walk and talk in your sleep. And worry about everything, like whether the dogs were being fed."

We laughed.

"You never did interview me," my mother said quietly.

I looked up at her, a question on my face.

"Like you interviewed your dad that time. Remember? When you were in graduate school at Smith and we came to visit you in Northampton," she said.

She clipped a thread on my father's pants with a small pair of orange-handled scissors.

"Oh my God, Mom," I said. "You're right. I wonder what happened?"

It took me off-guard that she was referring, not to my current work, but to an event which had happened more than three years earlier. In that time, I had moved to Chicago for a year's internship, then returned to Boston where I'd landed my first professional job as a social worker at Children's Hospital. And they had moved to Massachusetts.

I wondered what was on her mind that she'd be thinking about that interview with my father. Had Dad spoken to her about it? Had she been waiting for me to return to the so-called project so she could tell her side of the story?

"Would now be a good time to do it?" I asked tentatively.

"Sure. What do you want to know?" she asked. "You pretty much know everything about my history. I grew up in New Kensington, Pennsylvania. I had an older brother, Rich, a younger brother, Chuck and a sister, Pat."

She stopped and looked up at me. "Is this the way it is supposed to go?" she asked. Her jumping right in, almost as if she was giving a deposition, made me wonder what my father had told her about our talk.

"Yes, Mom. It's fine. Whatever way is comfortable for you to talk about yourself."

"Okay. My dad worked as a laborer in the Tube Mill for *Alcoa*. You know, it's where they made aluminum tubing."

She paused to light a cigarette. Being with my mother really made me want to light up. My whole body remembered this gesture, which signaled we were really about to dive into something. If I still smoked, I would have lit up with her, signaling back that we were in it together—whatever *it* was. A conspiratorial light-up. I felt bad making my mother hang out there on her own.

No. I couldn't. I'd quit more times than I can count. There would always be a good reason to light up.

As if she read my thoughts she asked, "Still not smoking?"

"Nope," I said. "Haven't had a cigarette in three months. Since my thirtieth birthday."

"You always said, 'I'll never quit quitting.' "

I laughed. I knew she was chiding me. If I never quit quitting it meant I was always failing, having to quit over and over again.

I breathed in her smoke as it wafted over me. "Ah, just one..."

No. I wouldn't give up this time.

As if she'd read my mind, my mother looked up at me as she slowly drew in a long inhale.

"Tell me about your childhood," I said. "Was it happy?"

From what I'd observed over the years, it didn't appear very happy to me, but I wanted to hear what she would say.

"In some ways it was happy," she said. "We had a lot of friends and

family around so we had a lot of fun. But it wasn't so much fun at home sometimes. Pappap really had a mean streak and made life miserable."

"Really?" I prodded.

"Oh, he was awful!" she said. "When he hollered, he expected all of us to jump. Your Gram waited on him hand and foot. But now I can see why she did. She would have done anything to hold the family together, because both of her parents had died when she was young... her father when she was eight and her mother when she was fourteen."

"Wow. I didn't realize that. Where did Gram go after that?"

"That's just it," she said. She went with Pappap. She met him at a Halloween party two weeks before she turned fifteen. Her mother died the day before her birthday. She married Pappap the following January."

"Like six weeks after meeting him?" I asked, amazed.

"Yep. He was an older man who could take care of her and her younger brothers. Pappap was nineteen," my mother said, laughing. "She had her first baby, Uncle Rich, on her sixteenth birthday, the following November."

"Oh my God. I never put it together how young Gram was," I said, "First her mom dies the day before her fifteenth birthday...is that right?"

My mother nodded.

"...and by the next birthday she has a baby! It's amazing to me that she and Pappap have stayed together all these years."

"I think that's because Gram was determined to hang onto her brothers and sister after their parents died," my mother said, tamping out her cigarette. "Believe me, Pappap wasn't an easy man to live with, for any of us. Especially when he was drinking... and that was just about all the time."

So much time had passed since I'd begun my exploration, I was too impatient to move slowly through her childhood up until the point of my birth. I jumped ahead.

"Let's talk about how you met Dad," I said.

"His family moved to our neighborhood when I was about thirteen... you know, just four doors down from Gram's. That big brown house? My best friend Zetta and her sister Liddy and I were checking out the family moving in and we saw they had an older boy in the family. He was a dreamboat! So, when it got to be time for school to start, we went to the house offering to walk the little kids to school. We acted as if we didn't know about the older brother. He came along, too."

"Smart girls! Did you like him right from the start?"

"I thought he was a real handsome guy, but I was kinda sweet on Zetta and Liddy's older brother at the time," she admitted.

We continued the interview, confirming my father's version, that he had run away to the Merchant Marines and then his brother had died.

"What made you contact Dad?" I asked.

"I don't know. I guess I knew the family wasn't going to. They were too upset," she said.

"How did you know how to send a telegram?" I asked.

"Gram knew how, and she helped me. It was the war years and telegrams were a common thing, especially getting telegrams with bad news."

"Is that how you learned Uncle Rich had died?" I asked.

My mother paused as she tied off a knot and cut the thread.

"Yes, but that was several years later. You were two years old."

She paused as she picked up a spool to thread another needle.

I could tell by my mother's face and by long history that this was an emotional subject for her. We rarely talked about Uncle Rich.

"That was really terrible. I'll never forget receiving the news that he was missing." she said.

My Aunt Pat, my mother's sister, had told me this story. She had been in her senior year of high school and had just come home from picking up her cap and gown for graduation when the phone call came. Her father told her to go and pick up her sister Harriet and the girls (my sister and me) and then go get her brother Chuck at school.

Pappap, their father, had dreamed of his son Rich, who was serving in the Navy at Narragansett Bay, Rhode Island several days before the phone call came. Pappap went to work the next morning and told his brother "something bad is going to happen to Rich." He told him the details he'd seen in his dream and his brother tried to explain it all away as worry.

A few days later, when the call came in, Pappap knew it was the Navy notifying the family that Rich was missing. Twenty-four days later, they found his body. When they delivered it for burial, the officers were about to tell the family the details when my grandfather interrupted them, "I know what happened. They had too many men on the launch that day and there was a storm. Rich was at the far end. He hit his head on the railing and was knocked unconscious as he fell into the water and drowned." The officers were astounded. The story was not only accurate, it provided even more detail than the story they'd been told.

"Pappap often had prophetic dreams, didn't he?" I asked.

"Yes, he did," she said. "He often woke up and told us he'd dreamed that somebody died, and sure enough, we'd get news that that person had passed away in the night. It got to the point where he stopped telling his dreams."

"Didn't he also dream of people after they died? I think Aunt Pat told me how they waited for Pappap to dream about Uncle Henry to know he had made it safely to the other side."

My mother nodded as she smoothed out the fabric on her lap.

"When I was young and heard these stories, they made me a little scared of Pappap," I said. "Like him blowing fire, I expected to see flames arising out of a person's burn."

My mother laughed. "I never thought about that... I don't know who named it blowing fire. Maybe because he blew *on* the fire, on the burn..."

———

"OWWWW!" Screams burst forth from the kitchen, accompanied by a crashing sound of metal meeting metal, followed by a softer thud.

"Dad, Dad! Come in here. Mom's burned herself!"

Heeding my mother's call to him, my grandfather quickly hoisted himself from his easy chair and moved to the kitchen, where my grandmother was holding her wrist and wincing in pain. The skin on the soft side of her arm was beet red, as was her face as she alternately held her breath and then exhaled in explosive, pain-driven puffs.

Pappap sat down on a small stool before her and calmly took her arm into his hands, resting it on his lap. He bent over and with near religious devotion he addressed his face to the burn and began to blow on it through his pursed lips. As he began, the room itself, it seemed, as well as all present, breathed a sigh of relief. My grandmother's face ceased its contortion and a few tears trickled down her cheek.

My grandfather was blowing fire.

I had seen him do this many times. I had experienced it myself. The only blister or scar I'd ever had from burns were from times when I was injured away from my grandfather. He had blown fire from major scaldings as well as from a hot coal falling on a foot. Once my grandfather blew, there was complete healing. I don't know where he learned to do this, but it was treated as sacred knowledge within my family.

This ability was one which had been passed down through generations, and for some unknown reason, it had to be passed across gender, with males teaching females, and then females the males. My mother learned it from my grandfather, my brother learned it from her. I felt bereft that being a girl rendered me ineligible to receive this unique and special gift.

It wasn't until I was in college that the obvious occurred to me. I could ask Pappap himself to teach me! On spring break, I went to visit my grandparents.

"Pappap, would you teach me to blow fire?"

I could see the solemn yet pleased look in his eye. My generation hadn't taken this skill as seriously as he would have liked. My cousins back in Pennsylvania hadn't learned, even though they'd had access to him every day. Perhaps they'd taken it for granted that they would always have him as their personal fire extinguisher. Or maybe they no longer believed. I'd heard that my cousin learned it from his mother but had never used it on his children.

"Yes, honey," Pappap had said. "I'll teach you."

He'd turned off the TV and took my hand in his. He told me it all centered on a particular Bible verse. This verse was his mental focus all the while he was blowing. He emphasized the importance of not breaking the concentration. He told me the verse. I repeated it to him several times. A warmth spread over me--a tender pride at having been initiated into a fellowship from which I had for so long felt excluded. It was a moment of unparalleled sweetness with Pappap--a moment of entering into a secret part of his world, bonding us in a new way.

Although my mother knew how to blow fire, I don't recall ever seeing her do it. But she herself had her own set of special powers, a way of knowing things.

When I was little, she had a foolproof way to learn if I was telling the truth or not. She would ask me to stick out my tongue and would make a great show of looking very carefully, reading the signs of my truthfulness right there in my open mouth. It wasn't until I was well into my grade school years that I realized it was my behavior that revealed whether or not I was lying. If I was telling the truth, I was all too eager to display my tongue. In fact, I would offer it voluntarily as proof of my honesty. When I was lying, I would seal my lips and turn my head away from her. Naturally, when she finally succeeded in getting me to open my mouth, she immediately read mendacity. She was right every time.

But her way of knowing things extended far beyond the observational and the deductive and went much further than tricking a gullible child.

One night when I was in my early twenties, I came home from college for a weekend visit. I had been out for the evening with friends, and when I arrived home, I found my brother Bill and his girlfriend in the family room watching Saturday Night Live while my parents were asleep upstairs. When the program was over, Bill got up to take Karen home. My car was the last car in the driveway so I tossed him my keys so he could use my car instead of me having to get up and move it.

Bill and Karen had been gone about twenty minutes when my mother came wandering sleepy-eyed down the stairs. She was surprised to see me there in front of the TV.

"Oh, Barb," she said. "I'm glad you're home. I just had a dream that you were stopped by a policeman at the top of the Commerce Street Bridge."

"No, I'm here. Got in about a half-hour ago."

"Okay. Goodnight. Will you be sure to lock up before you go to bed?"

"Sure, Mom. Goodnight."

Fifteen minutes later, Bill returned. As he tossed the keys onto my lap, he said, "Hey, Barb, did you know you have a busted taillight? A cop pulled me over at the top of the Commerce Street Bridge. Better get it fixed."

―――――

Once my mother had re-threaded her needle to move on to

a second pair of my father's pants, she put it aside while she lit another cigarette. She scrunched up her face as she took a long drag in, then slowly let it out and returned to her needlework.

"Mom, you got a bit of that gift from Pappap." I said. "Remember how you used to torment Dad by always being able to tell what he'd gotten you for Christmas?"

She laughed. "Yeah, that was funny," she said.

It was actually uncanny how she did that. Once he brought the package into the house, she knew what it was, even if she hadn't seen the package. One year he bought her the same thing for her birthday in November and then repeated the gift for Christmas. She knew it. They had a system where she would hand him a piece of paper on which she had written her impression before he gave her the package. My favorite was when he had bought her a watch. He asked her how many letters were in the word in her note. She said ten. He was psyched. He thought he'd finally outwitted her. He gave her the box and then opened the paper note.

Wristwatch, it said.

As I sat with my mother, remembering a lifetime of stories about her intuitive knowing, it occurred to me she must have knowledge about whether she gave birth to twins. Nothing else made sense.

"Do you still do that...guess your Christmas gift?"

"No," she said. "I purposely shut that down."

"Really?" I asked. "Why? How?"

"Because I didn't like knowing things that were going to happen."

Even as my mother said this, I had a flutter deep in my belly that made me wonder if she had in truth shut down her inner knowing on purpose or if she had just shut down letting anyone know what she knew. Or maybe when one doesn't want to know things, their system shuts down, consciously or not.

Ugh. I wish I could shut down this question. It has plagued me my whole life. Is it true, is it not, did they know, do they not, am I just crazy, did I make this up?

Suddenly my mind shifted to stories I had been told about my childhood which I had accepted as told ,but they weren't actually my memories.

Ah, yes. The doll with the purple dress.

When I was about three, apparently I had already established that my favorite color was purple. That Christmas, I asked for a doll with a purple dress. As the story goes, I unwrapped my present on Christmas morning and exclaimed, "Oh! Thank you so much for the doll with a purple dress!" Except it was a doll with a yellow dress. The story had always been told as a funny tale illustrating that I didn't really know what purple was, so I was happy with the yellow.

The older I got and the more I listened to my gut, I wondered if, in fact, I had known it was yellow but I had already figured out a way to not show disappointment at not getting what I wanted by converting everything into the fulfillment of my dream, to be the happy child my father praised me for being.

I wanted to move away from this memory when another one took its place. Around that age, maybe a little younger, there was another *cute* story about me. My mother and I (and maybe Joyce) were walking in downtown New Kensington when, holding my mother's hand, I stepped off the curb, almost into the pathway of an oncoming car. My mother managed to jerk me back and save my life just in time, but it resulted in dislocating my shoulder. I was taken to the doctor's and had to wear a sling for a period of time.

Whoever told the story always emphasized how *cute* it was, a teeny little girl wearing a sling. Although I don't actually remember the event, as I became older and learned to listen to my body, it screamed that this story was not true. The injury was true, the sling was true but there had never been an oncoming car or danger.

My body knows of my mother's frustration and rage. I've seen it all my life. I'm sure I stepped off the curb and made my mother angry. She yanked me and dislocated my shoulder. The strange thing is, I understand, and I even feel compassion for her. What I hate is the whitewashing, making the injury my fault and then turning it into a *cute* story. Every time I accepted one of those stories about me, I abandoned myself.

I felt tempted to ask my mother about this story as I watched her hem my father's pants, just to confirm my memory was correct and not how the story had been passed down. The wave of nausea which passed through my body reminded me not to invite this story ever again.

———

Although I imagine it was Mom who told me the Mrs. Wechsler story to begin with and helped me keep it alive since I was small, I had no memory of any conversation with her about it. I took a deep breath and plunged in.

"Mom, tell me about my birth."

She laughed and looked up from her sewing. "What do you want to know about your birth?" she asked.

"What's funny?" I asked.

"Oh, I was just laughing at the question. I don't really remember your birth because they knocked me out right before."

"They knocked you out before my birth? Why?"

"That's just the way they did it in those days, at least in the Navy," she said. "Then, as soon as you were born, they whisked you away and I didn't even get to see you for forty-eight hours."

"Because I was an RH baby?" I asked.

"Yes. They had to do a complete blood exchange." she said.

"I remember when you first told me that story when I was little," I said. "You told me they had to take out all my blood and put in new blood. I was freaked out because I thought they'd drained out all my blood and left me like a balloon with no air...just all skin lying there. And then they blew me back up with new blood. Then you told me that that wasn't the way they did it, that they took a teaspoon from my shoulder and put a new teaspoonful in my ankle, until all the old blood was out and the new blood was in."

She smiled. "I suppose you realize that's not exactly how they did it. They didn't really do it with a teaspoon."

I giggled. "Yeah. I figured that out by the time I was twenty or so. So what happened when you got me back?" I was definitely leading the witness. I knew what she was going to say, and I loved hearing it over and over again.

"Oh, when they brought you back to me, I took you and unwrapped you and looked you over, every little inch, just to make sure you were all there."

"That must have been tough on you...to have had a baby you didn't even get to see. A long forty-eight hours."

A silence fell between us as my mother refocused on her sewing.

I could tell by the way she was pulling the pins out of the fabric that she was getting irritated. I didn't know why, but I knew from long history not to ask her about it.

I started to panic. I had somehow already gotten her on the defensive and I hadn't even asked the most important questions.

"A lot of weird things happened at the hospital when I was born..." I began.

"That's true," she jumped in, seeming relieved to be on different territory. "Like when they delivered you to the wrong mother at feeding time. I was at the end of the line, and when they gave me the baby, I shrieked, 'This is not my baby!' They said, 'There, there, dear, of course, it's your baby.' They were treating me as though I was just a nervous mother. But I knew damned well that wasn't my baby. And it turned out, it wasn't! They had delivered you to another woman and she had already fed you!"

I winced. This part of the story always made me feel guilty that I had been such a disloyal and undiscerning infant. I had accepted succor at another woman's breast.

"But how could that happen?" I asked. "Didn't they have a system for keeping track of babies, like wristbands or something? And what about the fact that my birth certificate says I am a twin?"

There. It was out. I held my breath.

"Yeah, that's right," she said. "I feel kinda bad about that."

I looked at her quizzically.

"By the time we got your birth certificate, we had already moved back to Pennsylvania. I should have sent it back so they could correct it, but we were busy and it didn't seem important at the time." she said.

"When you got it, did it make you wonder if it might not be a mistake?"

"No. Why would I think that?"

"Didn't the doctor think you were going to have twins beforehand?" I asked.

"They couldn't tell if there were two heartbeats, or if you just had a very fast heartbeat."

"And didn't you gain a whole lot of weight?"

"The doctor I saw in my eighth month thought so. When I went for my check-up, he told me to either lose weight or find someone else to deliver my baby."

"What a bastard," I said.

"You know, if we weren't in the Navy and I could've gone to another doctor, I would have," she said.

"Wasn't there a story about a Mrs. Wechsler?" I asked.

"Oh, yeah. Mrs. Wechsler came in while I was in labor. The nurses were really worried about her because they thought she was going to lose her baby. She was already on the verge of a nervous breakdown and they were afraid if she lost the baby, it would really throw her over the edge," she said.

"You learned all this from the nurses?" I asked. "They actually told you all this?"

"No, of course not," she said. "I overheard them talking to each other."

"So what happened?" I asked.

"She was okay, I guess."

"Didn't you hear the nurses say the baby had died?" I asked.

"I thought I did," she said. "When I woke up in the

recovery room after you were born, I thought I heard a nurse say the Wechsler baby had died. I remember it because it made me think at first that *my* baby had died. But no, it was the Wechsler baby."

"But the Wechsler baby didn't die?"

"No," she said. "Back on the ward, I saw Mrs. Wechsler with her baby."

"But, what about what you heard in the recovery room?" I asked.

"I think it must've been something I imagined. They say under anesthesia you can hallucinate. Maybe I hallucinated hearing that because I had been worried about Mrs. Wechsler."

"Did you know her?"

"No. She was just another Navy wife, in to have her baby."

"That's what I thought. It's kind of amazing you remember her after all these years," I said.

"You think so?" she asked.

"Yeah, I do." I said. "Even I have remembered her my whole life, just from hearing the story. So when you got the birth certificate, what was it--three months later--did you think of Mrs. Wechsler?"

"No, why would I?" she asked.

"It never crossed your mind that maybe you had twins and when Mrs. Wechsler's baby died, they might have given her one of your babies?"

I couldn't believe these words had just come out of my mouth so smoothly and calmly. A part of me watched in disbelief, as if someone else was using my brain and my mouth.

My mother sat staring at me, not saying a word but not looking away.

"The reason I'm asking you this, Mom, is that I had a really unusual thing happen to me a couple of years ago." It suddenly struck me that my father had clearly not told her about our conversation about The Dinner Party and someone mistaking me for Kaye Wechsler.

"When I first moved to Boston, I met a woman who, upon meeting me, mistook me for someone from her home town. I later learned she was from Jacksonville and the person she said I looked exactly like was a person named Kaye Wechsler."

My mother sat silently, transfixed by what I had just told her. After a moment she said, "Wow. You should write this."

I was puzzled. "Write this?" I asked.

"It's just such an amazing story," she said.

FOR DAYS AFTER THE INTERVIEW, MY MOTHER'S WORDS reverberated in my ears.

You should write about it.

I was as baffled by my mother's response as I had been by my father's. What could she be saying? It hadn't been sarcastic or rejecting--it had been sincere. Why would she want me to write about it?

She'd seemed spellbound by the story. In fact, she'd been more interested and focused on what I was telling her than I had ever before known her to be. She was fully present as I told her about The Dinner Party and being mistaken for a Wechsler. But there was nothing in her manner which either confirmed her knowing the information to be true or refuting the story outright. Yet, she was the one, I was certain, that had told me the whole Mrs. Wechsler story when I was a young child.

And yet her response felt as though I was telling her a fascinating story which had nothing to do with her.

I hadn't thought it forward enough to imagine what my

parents would do with the information I was giving them. I had been so focused on my fear of telling them, my worry that the news would blow them apart or that they'd be angry at me for disturbing our family life, I hadn't thought about what reaction I'd anticipated. I'd had a child's perspective that upon hearing the story, they would swoop in and take action. I had thought they would understand, that they would be concerned and that they would help me. We'd be in this together. After my conversation with my mother, I knew I was on my own.

I began to tell the story to others at every opportunity, to my colleagues and my friends. As I became acquainted with people, I'd include the *twin mystery* in the getting-to-know-you phase of the relationship. It became a compulsion for me to do so and I realized after some time that I was trying to deputize as many people as I could to be on the lookout. My fantasy was that someone would hear my story, then run into you, Kaye, and would then connect us. I had told the story in several states. I really wanted the truth to come and find me in some irrefutable way, the same way the clues had come in the form of The Dinner Party. Unbidden. That way, I wouldn't be responsible for disrupting anyone's life.

It would be an act of God.

I kept telling the story with a secret wish that I would eventually tell it to someone who would say, "I can help you." Truth be told, I wanted someone to say, "Here, let me take care of that for you."

Women with children seemed most baffled by my mother's response. Not by the writing comment, but by the lack of strong refutation. More than one said to me, "You know, if my daughter came to me with this story, I would be able to say to her with absolute, reassuring certainty, 'No, you are not a twin. Believe me, I know. I was there.'"

I knew this was true. Although both of my parents said it was a mistake, neither said it with any clarity and conviction. Neither had a reassuring response. To the contrary, as the months and then the years went on, my parents responses became more and more distressing to me.

Several months after my conversation with my mother, my father's mother and Aunt Margaret came to visit and I went to my parents' house to have dinner with them. It was a pleasant meal with lively conversation about people back home and stories from the past.

As we began dessert, my father said, "By the way, Barb, I sent away for the hospital records from your birth. They had been sent to the federal records center in St. Louis. Unfortunately, I found out they destroy them after twenty-five years. Too bad. We missed them by just a few years."

"Oh," I said.

Actually, I already knew what he said was true, because by this time I had investigated it myself. On one hand, I was pleased with this evidence, discovering the situation had been on his mind and that he'd actually taken some action to help me discover the truth.

On the other hand, I couldn't understand why he would announce this at dinner with his mother and aunt present. I had never had a discussion about this with both of my parents together, much less extended family, and I was certain this wasn't a situation in which we could get into why I wanted to find my birth records.

After my father's announcement, we just went on with dinner, case closed.

Pass the potatoes.

From that evening on, I knew my father's goal was to put my search to rest rather than to help me find the truth, but I didn't know why. I knew I had two choices--forget the whole thing or go underground, taking the search into my own hands.

CHAPTER 16

JANUARY 1980

THE NEXT WINTER, SALLY AND I PLANNED A TRIP TO Disney World. As we prepared to go, she said to me, "I hope you're not intending to look for Kaye Wechsler while we're down there. If you are, you should do some groundwork. You can't just roam through the streets of Jacksonville hoping to see someone who looks like you."

"I know. Don't be silly," I replied. "Besides, Jacksonville is about four hours from Orlando. This is just a vacation."

Nevertheless, I knew I would be alert, trying to spot anyone who looked like me or anyone who seemed to recognize me. No matter where I traveled, I always carried a sense of possibility, a secret hope that fate would draw us into the same path. I was certain that someday I would find you, perhaps in the least likely place.

I looked in airports all over the world. I had lost the connection to Kim, the Jacksonville woman from The Dinner Party, so now whenever anyone said I looked like someone they knew, I pressed them for details. One obvious thing I'd neglected to ask Kim that night was your age. Such a simple detail which could have put this whole question to rest.

I was riveted to any TV story or magazine article having to do with lost relatives finding each other. I remember one in which two women were working in the bakery of a big discount department store. Over the years, they had become friends. Friend A knew she had a sister who had been taken from the family at birth and whom she was trying to find. Friend B understood the longing her friend had to connect because she herself had been adopted, but for some reason had never searched to find her biological family. When A's search ended, it turned out B was her sister, much to the surprise and delight of both.

I'd cry at every one of these stories. I prayed for something simple and irrefutable like that to happen to me, something which would make it so crystal clear I would no longer have to follow crumbs to find you. I wouldn't feel I was hurting my parents by needing to know the truth. They couldn't blame me if fate brought you back to me.

After an initial scouting around as we passed through the airport, I managed to put you out of my mind, and Sally and I had a carefree time at Disney World. Midweek, we decided to take it easy and just stay at our hotel for the day, reading by the pool and napping in the sun. Around noon, I became restless.

I sat up in a rush to speak. Sally looked at me expectantly. I hesitated.

"What's wrong?" she asked.

"I want to go to Jacksonville."

Sally rolled her eyes and turned back to her book for a second. She sighed.

"Okay," she said. "When? Tomorrow?"

"Now," I said.

Her eyes narrowed. I saw the little ripple in her jaw line, a sure sign that she was trying to clench her anger.

"Barbara, it's already noon..." She broke off, knowing it was impossible to dissuade me.

"I'll go by myself," I said.

For a brief second, I could see her considering letting me go alone.

"Don't be ridiculous." With a huff, she gathered up her book and towel.

"I'll drive," I said cheerily.

She gave me a look that let me know it would be preposterous for me to imagine otherwise.

I drove while Sally silently fumed. Occasionally, she'd let out a big sigh then dramatically turn her head toward the window, drumming her fingers on her left thigh. I tried to cajole her into a happy sense of adventure.

When that failed, I moved into obsequious attention to her comfort. Was the air conditioning cool enough? Did she want to stop for a drink?

She ignored my queries. Finally, she fell silent. I was hurt by her sullenness, her lack of support. Having to pay so much attention to her at this point felt like a burden.

After many miles, she broke the silence, mumbling about a wild goose chase. With that, the last little trickle of patience drained out of me.

"You are being such a pain in the ass! I know this seems crazy to you. I know this isn't the way you would do things. But under the circumstances, can't you just humor me?"

She was silent. She turned her face to the window.

"If you're just going to be such a pain, you should've stayed back at the hotel."

I felt a sensation of hot, cinnamon-scented steam filling my lungs, heading towards my mouth. "This is hard enough for me, Sally. Why do you have to make it harder?"

We returned to our separate silences. I continued my tirade silently for a while and then began to soften, realizing why Sally would be so distressed about my searching for you.

———

Eleven years earlier, back in her native Australia, Sally had been forced to give up a daughter at birth. Despite having come from a prominent family and having had a respectable life, because she was a lesbian, she was judged to be an unfit mother.

She had agonized over the separation. She had resolved to accomplish something that would one day make her daughter proud. She had emigrated to the United States and had taken an undergraduate degree at Harvard. She was currently working on a master's there.

Throughout the years, she had done what she could to leave a trail so her daughter could one day find her. Every year on the little girl's birthday, Sally wrote a letter to her that she mailed to herself. She saved these letters unopened, so if they were ever reunited, her daughter would have the postmarked evidence of her mother's love for her.

En route to Jacksonville, I focused on feeling compassion, knowing that Sally's anger was complicated and deep, and what I was doing was stirring it all up for her again.

But I couldn't let it stop me.

———

When we arrived in Jacksonville, I made a beeline for the Jacksonville Naval Hospital. As I drove through the gates, my heart pounded. Just being there felt like a betrayal. I fought my irrational fear that I would be caught and punished, as though I were a criminal trying to extract top-secret information. I reached the medical records office just as they were about to close for the day. They had confirmed what I had learned by mail, that all old hospital records had been sent to St. Louis for storage and then were destroyed after twenty-five years. There was nothing less satisfying than reconfirming an already established dead end.

Then inspiration struck.

"Do you know anything about high schools in this area?" I asked. "Where do kids who live on base go to school?"

"Well, there are several," the young woman began.

"Which ones," I interrupted her, "are old high schools--schools that would have been here in the sixties?"

She looked at me as if I was quizzing her on ancient history. "I'm not sure," she said. "But you might try Forrest High. It's over on Firestone Road."

I returned to the car, where Sally was slouched in the front seat.

"God, what are you sitting in the hot car for!?" I asked. "You are going to get brain damage."

She gave me a dirty look and said, "I don't think I'm the one with the brain damage."

I told her my idea to find a high school in order to see if I could get access to a yearbook. Sally interrupted brusquely.

"I'm hungry," she said.

We pulled into the Pizza Hut. I was worried that it was

past four o'clock and the school would be shutting down for the day, and I knew I wouldn't be able to get Sally to hang around overnight. Her resistance seemed to get heavier and heavier. I sensed her investment in this being a failed venture. I could practically see *I told you so* outlined on her lips.

While Sally ordered, I went outside to the pay phone stuck to the side of the brick building. I could hardly hear the dial tone as trucks zoomed by on the highway.

"HI!" I hollered. "I'M SORRY FOR SPEAKING SO LOUD. I'M OUT BY THE HIGHWAY. WOULD YOU MIND SPEAKING UP, TOO?"

"OKAY," I heard. "HOW CAN I HELP YOU?"

"DID YOUR SCHOOL EXIST IN 1967?"

"YES."

"I'M LOOKING FOR OLD YEARBOOKS FOR 1964-1967."

Even to my own ears, I was sounding like a hyped-up nutcase. I couldn't believe this woman was putting up with this.

"LOOK, I KNOW THIS SOUNDS ODD, BUT I HAVE REASON TO BELIEVE I HAVE A TWIN SISTER FROM WHOM I WAS SEPARATED AT BIRTH, AND I THINK SHE WENT TO YOUR SCHOOL IN 1967. I'D LIKE TO SEE A PICTURE OF HER."

There. I'd blurted out the whole truth. It sounded even more nutty. The line went silent when I finished. I strained to see if I could hear a dial tone, certain the woman had hung up. Then I heard her voice explaining that she didn't think the school kept its old yearbooks on-site, but she had an idea. Jerry Jackson, the football coach and English teacher, had graduated from Forrest in the late '60's. Maybe he could help us.

US? Yes, she had definitely said *us*. It was the sweetest sound I had ever heard.

"GREAT!" I exclaimed with a purpose beyond volume.

"LET ME SEE IF HE IS STILL IN THE BUILDING. DO YOU WANT ME TO CALL YOU BACK?"

I PANICKED. Oh, this is how she'll get rid of me. I didn't want to let her go.

"I DON'T KNOW IF THIS PHONE TAKES INCOMING CALLS. CAN I CALL YOU BACK?"

"OKAY. I'M SHERRY. CALL BACK IN TWENTY MINUTES."

I hung up. I paced back and forth as if I was tethered to the building by a short leash. I didn't want to go inside to Sally for fear I would get lost trying to make her feel better and thereby lose my determination to keep going with my pursuit.

I looked up to see a man coming in my direction. I didn't want him to touch that phone. I quickly picked up the receiver as though I were about to make a call. The man continued on past me, got in his car and drove away.

Suddenly I had an idea for filling the time. I lifted the dog-eared telephone book hanging by the cable and quickly thumbed to the W's. There were twenty-seven Wechslers.

"HELLO. I'M TRYING TO REACH KAYE WECHSLER..."

"WHAT? WHAT? WHO IS THIS?"

"THANK YOU."

I hung up and moved to the next.

"HELLO. I'M TRYING TO REACH KAYE WECHSLER."

"SORRY, HONEY. I NEVER HEARD OF HER."

Again.

"HELLO. I'M TRYING TO REACH KAYE WECH-SLER. IS SHE A MEMBER OF YOUR FAMILY?"

"LET ME GET STUMPY."

Uh-oh. This didn't sound good.

I considered hanging up when I heard the rummaging sound of someone trying to get the phone to their ear.

Oh my God, it was bad enough I'd disturbed him. How could I hang up?

"HELLO, STUMPY? I'M TRYING TO FIND KAYE WECHSLER."

"WHO IS THIS? KAYE WHAT? NOBODY HERE BY THAT NAME". CLICK.

And so it went, my throat becoming tighter with each call, the little waif in my belly trying harder to crawl out. Or cry out. I looked through the window and saw Sally slumped in the booth, her head in her hands.

Should I go in? I glanced at my watch. Seven more minutes until I could call Sherry back. I let out a deep sigh and found the next number in the phone book. After three more rejections, it was time to call Sherry.

"Hi, Sherry. Any luck?"

"Yes," she said. "He'd already gone for the day, but I reached him at home. He's coming back later for football practice. He said he'll bring his yearbook and he'll meet with you after practice. Around seven. Is that okay?"

"Yes," I said. "Thank you Sherry. I'll be there at seven."

And thank you, God, for the generosity of strangers who have no idea how much they help.

———

I was thrilled with the developments of the day. Needless to say, Sally was not. She did not relish killing two and a half hours at the Pizza Hut. I was so taken up with my own mission I couldn't see that her uncharacteristic bad humor was evidence of her rising distress.

I waited in the school office, a brightly lit oasis at the front of a massive building. The school was eerily empty on this dark January evening.

Jerry Jackson strode in, whistling, carrying a yearbook under his arm. His casual, confident air was the perfect antidote to my nervous intensity.

"Hi. Are you the lady who wants to look at my yearbook?"

Suddenly overcome by shyness, I smiled and nodded.

"Well, here it is," he said.

As he placed it on the counter, my heart sank.

1966.

"Who was it you wanted to look up?"

"Kaye Wechsler," I said. "Did you know her? I think she may have graduated in 1967."

"Oh, too bad. Let's just check and make sure she is not in here."

He began thumbing through the senior pictures. As he passed through the J's he impishly pointed out his own grinning likeness. He pointed to the picture next to his and said, "Here's my twin brother, Joe."

I smiled as he sped on to the W's. "No. No Kaye Wechsler. Too bad. The name is familiar but I can't place her. Why are you looking for her?" he asked.

"She is possibly my twin sister taken away at birth."

"What a coincidence," he said. "Did I tell you I'm a twin myself?"

"Yes, you showed me Joe's picture," I reminded him.

"Oh, right." he said.

I thanked him for his efforts.

"Wait. Let's not give up yet," he interrupted. "I'm wondering if the library has any old yearbooks in it. Or maybe in Christine Jacob's room. She's our yearbook editor and has been around forever. Let's see if we can get in there."

We walked down the dark corridor, the echo of our footsteps the only sound. I feared we were going to get caught until I reminded myself that I was no longer a kid and I was with a teacher. We searched the library to no avail.

"Let's go down to Christine's classroom," Jerry suggested.

As we neared an intersection in the corridor, I distinguished footsteps other than ours. My heartbeat quickened and my mouth went dry. A second later, a plump blond woman in her forties stepped out of the darkness.

"Christine! Glad to run into you!" Jerry said. "We were just on our way to your room to see if we could find some old yearbooks." Jerry went on to explain who I was and the purpose of our request.

"Oh," she said softly. "I don't have a '67 yearbook here, but I do have one at home. Can you come back tomorrow?"

I thought of Sally disintegrating in the front seat of the rental car.

"I'm sorry, but no. I have to be in Orlando tomorrow and then I'm flying back to Boston."

"Maybe you could leave your address and I'll check for

you. You know, I do remember teaching a Kaye Wechsler. Her real name was Brenda Kaye Wechsler, but she always went by Kaye."

I was amazed at and grateful for this woman's memory.

"Actually, Kaye moved her senior year," Christine said. "Yes. That's right. She was here at the beginning of the year but then her family moved to Miami, I believe. So her picture'd be in the yearbook, but I don't believe she graduated here."

I couldn't believe my luck. If I had written the school instead of visiting, they would have had no record of her as an alum.

I gave Christine my address and phone number back in Boston and thanked her for any help she could offer. As I wrote down the information, she spoke to Jerry.

"Maybe we could pull Nancy Martinson in on this." She went on to explain that Nancy was on the administrative staff and had helped a number of adopted kids find their birth parents.

"She may have some ideas that can help us," Christine said.

There it was again. *Us.* That magic word. A feeling of warm, sweet, all-you-can-eat pudding flowed down my gullet into my gut.

These southerners sure had an inclusionary charm.

———

The next day, Sally and I recuperated from our four-hour-round trip by once again lounging around the the hotel's pool. Sally was quieter than usual but no longer hostile. She appeared to be relieved the ordeal was over. I tried to be particularly attentive to her needs, grateful in the end that she had accompanied me despite her distress.

As Sally read a book, I mulled over the events of the day before. On the way back to Orlando, it had dawned on me that even if Kaye wasn't in the senior class of 1966, she still could have been in that book as an underclassman. I kicked myself mentally for not thinking of that the day before.

What a big leap I'd made! Kim had said I looked like you. I had never asked her your year of graduation. If you had been in the class of 1966, this whole wild goose chase would be over. You weren't in that class, but it didn't mean you were in the class of 1967, as I had been.

I really started to feel foolish. What if I found out you weren't anywhere near my age? If only I had asked Kim that night, I could have saved myself years of anxiety and confusion.

I thought back to the night before, to Christine Jacob's incredible recall. If she had such a good memory, why hadn't I asked her if I looked like you? Or why didn't she volunteer that information if it were true?

It seemed every time I got a little bit closer, my brain failed me and I'd manage not to get a crucial bit of information.

How frustrating.

What if I finally find you and it's *not* true? That question was with me then and it haunts me now. Somehow, this question is harder for me to contemplate than the reverse. What would it take for me to believe it's not true?

I glanced over at Sally, sitting serenely under her sun hat. No wonder she'd been so furious. I had been making a gigantic fool of myself.

Just then, I heard a phone ring. Feeling an urgency

inside. I looked up toward our door on the second-floor balcony on the opposite side of the courtyard. I tried to talk myself down. There's no way that could be our phone. It was too far away and there was nothing to distinguish our phone from any of the fifty others surrounding this courtyard.

I didn't dare react to the impulse to run for the phone. Sally had had enough of my erratic behavior. Besides, I reassured myself, the only other person who knew where we were was the dogsitter back home.

By the third ring, I was out of my chair.

"That's our phone," I said and went running as fast as I could up the stairs and down the corridor. I burst into the room and scooped up the receiver.

"Hello?"

"Hello. I'm looking for Barbara McCollough," the voice on the other end said.

"Speaking," I puffed into the phone.

"This is Nancy from Nathan B. Forrest High School."

Nancy had gotten the story from Christine, who'd called our home in Massachusetts and gotten our number in Orlando from the dog sitter. Nancy wanted me to know they'd found yearbook pictures of Kaye *Class of '67*.

Nancy said she would photocopy the pages and send copies of the senior picture as well as the underclass ones. She went on to tell me that she herself was adopted and had searched and found her birth mother. She said she understood my need to know my birth history and was happy to be of any help she could. She had already confirmed through Central Records that Kaye had not graduated from Forrest but had moved to Miami. She said she couldn't press further without arousing suspicion as to why she, a school administrator, wanted information on a student from so long ago.

She suggested a strategy for me to pursue.

CHAPTER 17

FEBRUARY 1980

I RETURNED FROM THE FLORIDA TRIP EXHAUSTED. I KNEW it wasn't from all the sightseeing and certainly not from lazy days hanging around the pool. I felt a familiar heaviness, a feeling on some level that life was just too much for me.

Grateful as I was that I had made connections with people in Florida who could help me find you, I felt even more alone with my dilemma. I had come to recognize the pattern. At each turn of the story, I'd hope for resolution, a dramatic moment when you would step out from behind the curtain and my search would finally be over.

Obviously, that never happened.

The search more resembled a hike up a very steep curving road. As I rounded each curve, thinking I had reached the top of the hill, I would see another hill ahead. True, it always felt good to have companions along for pieces of the journey, but inevitably it came to a point where I had to leave them behind and go on alone.

I was tired. And lonely.

And the truth was, I felt too little.

Anything I did regarding searching for you threw me into a childlike state of mind. I felt fearful. I felt as if I wasn't supposed to be doing what I was doing, so I felt like a bad girl. Inside, I was whining.

My colleague Jenny asked me how I was doing with the search. I told her, and also confessed to feeling helpless and alone.

She laughed. "Of course, you feel helpless and alone! That's exactly how you felt the last time you saw her!"

It took me a minute to get what she was saying. When I did, I started laughing. "Yeah, I guess I did. And I couldn't very well run after her then!"

But I still didn't like feeling this way. A cranky, angry, helpless baby. It was easier all around just to forget about it. Until this feeling went away. Until it started gnawing at me again. And then I'd do another round of searching for as long as I could stand feeling bereft and abandoned and that there was no one in the world who could help me.

About a week after returning home from Florida, I was back to my fully-functioning self. Back to work—busy, busy, busy.

Then the pictures arrived.

There was nothing about the large manila envelope that would indicate what was inside. A simple return address with no name. It's a wonder it didn't get discarded as junk mail.

But I opened it and there you were, page after page of photocopies from a yearbook—headshots of you in successive years, as well as you within groups to which you belonged.

As I looked at each page, I felt complete stillness, with the exception of the movement of my wrist as I turned each page. It was as if I believed that if I was really still, I could transport myself into the world on the page, that I would be able to feel you, to touch you, to hear your voice. And if I stirred even a little bit, I would be sent back to my world. It didn't work, and too soon I was simply in the kitchen looking at mail.

I don't know what I'd expected it would be like, getting the photos. Maybe that it would be a surprise being unveiled. I suppose a part of me thought you would look like a beautiful fairy princess.

I was disappointed. You looked kind of ordinary. You looked like me.

Kinda.

I wasn't sure. I considered Xeroxing my fifteen-year-old yearbook pictures to make a fair comparison. Your nose looked broad like mine. You had smallish dark eyes like mine. Even a stupid smirk, just like mine in my ninth-grade picture. Your senior picture looked the most like mine.

I think.

Is that what I looked like?

I really didn't know.

I didn't show anyone the pictures right away. I felt sick to my stomach when I looked at them, which I did twenty times a day. I carried them around with me in my notebook. I'd take them out at every private moment.

I still couldn't tell.

Did she look like me?

I didn't sleep for the next three nights.

For the first time since I'd started, this whole search felt weird to me. Really weird. Imagine, if you are not my sister, how strange it is that I have fixated on you my whole life, this person I don't even know. I imagined someone out there doing that about me, tracking down my teachers at Robert E. Lee High School. Staring at my pictures from the yearbook. It gave me the creeps.

I heard the story of a woman named Sandra whom I'd met at a summer workshop. She'd been adopted, and when she was pretty young, her adoptive mother thrust a book into her hands and said, "Read this. Then you'll understand about your real mother."

It was Park Avenue, a Harold Robbins novel about a call girl. This happened to be around the time of the Profumo sex scandal in Britain and there was a lot in the newspapers about Christine Keeler, an alleged call girl involved in the scandal. My acquaintance became convinced that Christine Keeler was her real mother. She began to keep a Christine Keeler scrapbook and had highly developed fantasies about being reunited with her beautiful, prostitute mother.

When she told the story, I understood exactly how she felt. I assume I am one of the few, if not the only person, in the world with a Kaye Wechsler scrapbook.

Sandra went on to find her mother, who turned out to be anything but a beautiful, sexy woman. She agreed to meet my friend, but my friend had to pretend she was a colleague from work in front of her mom's children and husband. When she met her, she found her birthmother to be crude and insensitive--and worst of all, needy.

My stomach churned as I looked at your photos. *Leave well enough alone* was having a vicious fight with *can't stop now!*

———

"Ugh!" I grunted as I pulled down the heavy volume from

the shelf in the Boston Public Library. The phone book for Miami, Florida. I flicked through the headings...ah, there, page 367, Dade County Schools...senior high schools. I began copying the list of twenty-seven addresses until it occurred to me this probably wasn't top-secret information and I could much more easily photocopy the whole page. By the end of the week, I'd sent out twenty-six letters using the tactic suggested by Nancy.

Dear Sir or Madam,

I am attempting to find a person whom I believe is a former student of yours by the name of Brenda Kaye Wechsler. Kaye, as she was called, was a friend of my sister's at Nathan B. Forrest High School in Jacksonville. However, in the middle of her senior year, Kaye moved to the Miami area and would have graduated in the class of 1967.

My sister passed away this year after a long illness. Before she died, she asked me to pass on a small gift of sentimental, more than material, value to her old friend Kaye.

In the emotional turmoil of those days, I neglected to obtain the current address and to inquire if Kaye had a married name. Since my sister's death, we have been unable to locate any information that includes Kaye's current address.

I know this may sound like an unusual request. However, I would greatly appreciate any help you can give as to where I might find Kaye. Would your alumni association have a current mailing address?

Thank you in advance for any help you can provide.

Sincerely,
Danielle Buchman

———

Dan Buchman was my apartment mate at the time. I was too paranoid to use my real name, certain they already had an all-state alert in Florida which prohibited anyone from responding to any request about Kaye Wechsler from a Barbara McCollough.

I received seven answers. Two of the seven had information about you. They said you'd entered Miami Palmetto Senior High School on October, 1965, where you'd attended for five months and then withdrew to return to Jacksonville on March, 1966.

This was different information from what I had been told at Forrest High. Was there no record of you graduating from there, or had it been overlooked?

Why would a student attend a different school for five months? It made me think of my sister Joyce. Come to think of it, didn't Joyce give birth in March, 1966? Or maybe it was '67.

I was sure there were other possibilities for why a young woman would split up her high school years. I looked forward to learning the real story.

But as interesting as this new information was, it brought me no closer to actually finding you. And that's all that mattered to me, not becoming an expert on your history. I felt as if the tears that had been locked in my throat for so long were now spreading to my lungs, making it hard to breathe.

I wasn't at all sure I would get to the finish line.

CHAPTER 18

1982

MY MOTHER SCRAPED THE GRAVY FROM THE FRYING PAN onto the porkchops as I held the plate up to her.

"Yum," I said. "That smells SO-O good!"

As we settled around the dinner table, my father said, "I have some news for you."

"Really?" I said. "What is it?"

"I'm retiring."

"Wow! But you're only fifty-five."

"Right. But I'm eligible and it's time for me to get out of the government grind. Your mother and I are going to get an RV and travel the country until we decide where we want to settle next."

I thought this sounded like a lot of fun and was happy for them, but it was hard for me to think about them leaving. It had been a difficult adjustment for me when they'd moved to the Boston area, but I had become accustomed to having them around and hated to see them go. Besides, Sally and I had recently split up and I was still adjusting to being alone.

Now my parents were leaving. I felt abandoned.

One day my mother and I went shopping, and as we drove back to her house, she gave me the running report of the preparations for the move. She told me about all the items she'd gotten rid of via their huge garage sale or through being tossed into the trash.

"I even got rid of those cows you gave me," she said.

"What cows?" I asked.

"You know, those two little ceramic cows you gave me for Mother's Day when you were about four?" She looked at me for confirmation.

"No, I don't remember any cows..." I began.

She let out a sigh of mock exasperation.

"Aunt Pat took you shopping at the five-and-ten and you were allowed to pick out your own gift for me for Mother's Day. You chose this little figurine...it's two cows in one figurine. They're huddled together."

I was still puzzled.

"Oh, for heaven's sake." my mother said, exasperated. "I'll dig them out of the trash when we get home so you can see them."

"Here they are," she said, handing me the small faded figurine. "Now do you remember?"

I took the object in my hand. I didn't know if I really remembered it, but it seemed familiar nonetheless. It fit nicely in the palm of my hand. A cheap, ten-cent tchotchke. Two little cows sitting on their haunches, their bodies so close you couldn't distinguish one from the other. Their two heads jutted out of their collective body at jaunty angles. One had a little flower behind its ear. And each had a goofy expression on its face.

"Awww...this is cute," I said. "I don't remember it,

though. Don't throw it away. I'll keep it."

As I drove home, I put the little cows on the flat section of the dashboard. I felt sentimental about the cows and about this change in my parents' life. It seemed irrational to feel so upset that they were leaving me. I wanted the cows as a memento of our long history together, rescued from the trash. I wondered why, of all the things I'd given my mother as a child—the funky refrigerator drawings, the handmade arts and crafts from school or scouts, had she kept these little cows? Most of this type of memorabilia had been culled during the twenty-some moves we had made as a family. I was touched and surprised that she would keep this cheap little ornament.

A few days later, Jenny came over and saw the figurine sitting on the coffee table in my living room.

"What's this?" she asked.

"Oh, it's a little thing I bought for my mother for Mother's Day when I was around four. She was going to throw it out, so I took it," I said.

"Twin cows?" she asked. "You gave your mother twin cows for Mother's Day?"

She stood there, cows in hand, with a look of incredulity on her face.

God. Twin cows.

I felt stupid that this hadn't even occurred to me.

Something in me woke up that day. Or at least I started to notice how asleep I'd been to major clues about your probable existence. The more I pondered my mother's saving those cows, the more I began to see how your ghostly presence operated between my mother and me and obviously had for a very long time. I also realized when I dropped the search, believing I was getting carried away with it, my mother inserted something new. Did she have any idea why she had saved the cows and no other child-hood gift from me? Did she wonder at all why she needed to tell me about them rather than just let them slip away with the trash?

I started to notice, often through the observations of friends, how my perspective on certain things was different from theirs and potentially reflective of being a twin. For example, BJ told a whole group of us about her experience in a flotation tank. She had gone to the Aqua Retreat Center and floated, as they called it, in an egg-shaped container filled with water with a very high saline content. We were all fascinated and pelted her with questions.

"What does it feel like?"

"What do you hear?"

"Does the salt burn your eyes?"

"Can you take someone in with you?"

After my question the momentum stopped.

"Ooooh. Weird. Why would you want to...like to have sex or something?"

I was embarrassed that I had asked a perverted-sounding question. I wasn't really thinking of anything in particular. It was just a naturally-occurring question to me.

It wasn't until later that Jenny, the keen observer, brought it up.

"Barb, I didn't want to say anything in front of the group, but your question wasn't so weird, really. After all, they claim this flotation tank is a simulation of being in the womb, so it makes sense to me that you would wonder if someone could be in there with you."

"Oh, right," I said. "I hadn't thought of that."

Embarrassed once again for my lack of insight, I

wondered how many more things like this were embedded in my consciousness and how, without Jenny, I would ever see any of them on my own.

One day, as I played doll house with a five-year-old girl on the inpatient unit of the hospital, I was transported back to myself at that age, when my best friend Samantha and I had learned to dance.

Samantha was a soft, plush doll with brown yarn hair. We were the exact same height, and although Samantha couldn't lead, she could follow my lead perfectly because she had elastic loops on her palms and the soles of her feet which slipped over my hands and feet. Most mornings after she came, we spent time together in the front room of the house. Sometimes we danced face to face. Sometimes I strapped her on, her back to my front and we colored together, me peeking over her shoulder to see the coloring book.

I spent a lot of time experimenting with ways we could do things as one. Sometimes I played my invisible game, hiding behind Samantha, pretending only she was in the room, imagining what she would be like if she didn't need me in order to walk around. I always wished she could talk.

Until that morning playing on the unit, I hadn't remembered Samantha. I began to wonder—where had she come from? Who had selected this particular gift for me as a child? What did the adults in my life make of my play with Samantha?

Was my memory correct in telling me Samantha came into my life right after my stay in the hospital when I was officially diagnosed as the worrywart my parents had suspected me of being? Was it Samantha who'd stopped my headaches, stomachaches and hand-wringing?

CHAPTER 19

1982 CONTINUED

SEEING THOSE TWIN COWS IN A NEW LIGHT, AND remembering Samantha, led me to wonder what other clues might be registered inside me about our relationship, if only I could unearth them.

At the time I'd gone to graduate school I had been studying humanistic psychology on my own and expected that when I got to Smith I'd be learning more in this area.

However, the first month at Smith, I'd found the curriculum a little dry. I'd said to my dormmate Celeste, "I can't wait 'til we get to studying Carl Rogers."

Celeste looked at me with a mixture of surprise and derision. "Are you kidding? We're never going to be studying Carl Rogers. This is a psychoanalytically-oriented program."

I tried to hide that I really didn't know what she was talking about.

"You know, Freud and the unconscious?" Celeste continued. "I don't think Sigmund and Carl were colleagues."

I felt so-o-o dumb.

And then again, not really. Celeste's comment shocked me back to my roots.

When I was a sophomore in high school, in English class we were

introduced to the mechanics of writing a term paper. We could select any topic we wanted as the focus for our project. Mine was entitled "A Brief Study of Psychoanalysis" and in its eventual ten-pages, a very confident fifteen-year-old spelled out the essence of the method in which "the patient lays down and the psychoanalyst unravels the past that is buried within the patient and once he does the patient no longer suffers from the problem." My impressive resources included a brochure from Metropolitan Life Insurance.

Around that time, I also learned about psychosomatic medicine as part of health class. So even though my path through college, marriage and divorce had led me to humanistic psychology, alternative self-help and the pursuit of the spirit, my unconscious choice of graduate programs had been totally in keeping with my earliest interest in that which lies deep in the human psyche.

I came to appreciate the foundation in the depth psychology I learned, first Freudian and then Jungian. Both are founded on the realization that we are way more than we think we are within our conscious mind. In fact, our conscious mind is only 5-10% of our awareness. The vast unconscious, that 90-95% which operates below our awareness is what really runs the show. We can't access the unconscious directly because, by definition, it is what is outside of our awareness, but it gives us hints all the time in our dreams and in our behaviors.

Carl Jung famously said, "When an inner situation remains unconscious, it appears outside as fate."

If that is the case, the truth about whether I was a twin must have been hidden in plain sight throughout my life, I thought, like the twin cows and Samantha. I began to contemplate other elements which could have been signs.

My first boyfriend, when I was in the sixth grade and living in Bauxite, Arkansas, was Bob Lewis. He was a dreamboat and, in my eyes, he was easily distinguishable from his twin Bill.

Oh my. Was that when I learned about Chang and Eng?

Even as a young girl, I loved to read and enjoyed reporting on my current book to my family at dinner. I came upon a book in the library about P.T. Barnum and learned he had a sideshow of conjoined twins (called Siamese twins then because these two came from Thailand, then known as Siam). I was riveted on the experience of these twins, telling my family all the facts I'd learned--they were joined at the sternum and couldn't be separated. They had different personalities and were said to have hated each other. They never agreed on anything. When one wanted to go to bed, the other wanted to sit by the fire. One of them was an alcoholic. They fathered twenty-one children between them and alternated living with their families every three days. Plus, they died twelve hours apart. I was obsessed with what that must have been like, living with a dead body attached to you, knowing you were going to die soon.

As I remembered this part, I could practically hear my father's words. "Okay, that's enough, Barb."

That makes me laugh, Kaye. Those words are practically

engraved on my eardrums I heard them so often. I always had something to go on about.

In my college days at Penn State, I joined a sorority, and when it was time to choose a little sister, I chose one of the only set of twins in our group. It was clear to me that my perfect match was Libby and not her identical sister Kathy.

One of the first courses I took in college was Greek 26. Expecting a language course, I was surprised to find it was mostly mythology. I selected the myth of the twins Castor and Pollux for my term paper. Looking back, I think I may have chosen them because they're connected to the constellation of Gemini, the twins, which is my birth sign (our birth sign). The story of Castor and Pollux is that Castor was mortal and Pollux was immortal. When Castor died, Pollux begged his father, Zeus, to allow him to share his immortality to keep them together. In accord with his desire, they were transformed into the constellation Gemini. When we look up at the sky, there they are, together forever.

The more I explored my memories, the more evidence I saw of a twin theme running throughout my life just beneath the surface.

I can't wait to find out if this has been true for you as well. If the reports on twins reared apart are accurate, then chances are, Kaye, your life is a lot like mine.

———

In 1979, Dr. Tom Bouchard, a psychology professor at the University of Minnesota, saw an article from the local newspaper about identical twins named Jim (Jim Springer and Jim Lewis) who had just met for the first time at the age of 39. Dr. Bouchard had been interested in studying twins reared apart but had no idea how he could find them. He seized upon the opportunity to interview the Jims.

They had been born in Ohio and had been adopted by different families when they were a few weeks old. Each of the adoptive parents were told their child's twin had died at birth. However, Mrs. Lewis learned the truth when she went to the courthouse to complete the adoption process. The clerk of the court had said to her, "You can't name him James, because they named the other little boy James."

When the twins were reunited in adulthood, they'd learned that each of them had married a woman named Linda, had been divorced and then had married a Betty. Their firstborn children were James Alan and James Allen. They each had a dog named Toy, they spent family vacations on the same beach in Florida and they both enjoyed mechanical drawing and carpentry. They were the same height and weight and each worked part-time in law enforcement. They each liked Miller Lite beer and chain-smoked Salem cigarettes.

Reading about them made me wonder if you and I have such similarities. Maybe you are a clinical social worker in private practice, have a dog named Scout and always keep a glass of water by your bed for fear of choking in the night. Maybe you are a self-help junkie, a spiritual seeker or like Haagen-Dazs and hate beets. Or maybe I keep a glass of water by my bed because you had a bad near-choking experience even though I never have.

I look forward to hearing how our histories line up.

CHAPTER 20

1984

SIX MONTHS AFTER MY PARENTS LEFT ON THEIR
retirement journey, they completed their travels and settled
in Florida.

We sat at the same butcher block table, the very same
one where I'd come out to them, and the one at which I'd
interviewed my mother about our family history. Only this
time, the table was in my Cambridge apartment, an item I'd
claimed when they'd purged themselves of their houseful of
furniture.

This time, they were visiting me.

I enjoyed the pace of their week-long visit. Something
about the periodic, complete immersion invited a different
kind of relating than when they'd lived in the area and we'd
squeezed each other in for Sunday dinner once or twice a
month.

We completed our errands and then rewarded ourselves
with a brisk walk around Fresh Pond, taking in the fall
foliage. When we returned to my apartment, we relaxed in

the kitchen, drinking tea and talking. They brought me up to date on the recent visit to our extended family back in Pennsylvania.

"We spent a day with Aunt Margaret," my mother said. Aunt Margaret was my paternal grandmother's youngest sister, just eight years older than my father.

"Yeah, that was really nice," my father said. "I don't ever remember spending so much time with her by herself. We talked about stuff nobody in my family has ever talked about."

"Really?" I asked. "Like what?"

"Oh, we talked about her and Gramma's life when they were little girls. You know, don't you, that they had different fathers? Their mother was married three times, so there were actually three sets of kids," he said.

I kind of knew this but could never keep the three fathers straight. I had never known any of that family except Gramma and Aunt Margaret, so the story didn't engage much of my interest.

My father leaned in closer towards the center of the table, his hands enfolding the large mug of tea. He looked me intently in the eye.

"You know, Barb, Aunt Margaret said something which just blew me

away," he said. "After this great visit we'd just had together, as we were wrapping things up, she said, 'I'm so glad we didn't get rid of little Billy.'"

He stopped, looking at me expectantly. Obviously, I wasn't getting the significance.

"She was saying," he went on, "that she was glad my mother had me and kept me instead of either having an abortion or giving me up for adoption." He had tears in his eyes. "Boy," he said. "Can you imagine? I never knew they'd ever considered giving me away."

A surge of feeling swept over me. I braced myself, attempting to remain upright in the tide, trying in the moment to do an instant sorting. On one hand, I felt love and compassion for my father. I was touched that he would share this vulnerable experience with me.

And yes, I did know how it felt. And I was furious.

"Gee, Dad," I said, my voice quivering. "It must have been very painful to realize you might've been separated from your family, or even not have been born."

As I paused for breath, I noticed his eyes softening, which only made me angrier.

"But you know, Dad," I went on, "it's hard for me to hear your story, since you *do* know how it feels. It really hurts me that since I told you what I've learned about the Wechsler baby, you have done nothing to help sort it out. Nothing!"

My throat tightened to the point of pain, as if I'd accidentally swallowed a shard of glass. I reached out for the cup in front of me. Neither of my parents spoke.

"It's not just about me," I continued. "It's about our family. And you have shown no interest. So, don't you see? If it's true, it means I could just as easily have been the one given away as the other baby. And you don't even care!"

I was ashamed to hear how shrill and urgent...and young... I sounded.

"That's not true," my father protested. "I tried to get the birth records. They'd been destroyed. What else can we do?"

"I don't know," I said, again hearing that little girl in my voice, hoping the adults would hear her and know what to do. "I don't know what to do or even if there is anything any of us can do. But I keep trying. You have shown no interest at all. You have never even brought it up. You know how I've suffered over this and you don't even seem to care." Again, my stomach churned, hearing that little child begging her parents to care.

My father started to respond but my mother interrupted.

"She's right, Bill. We haven't done anything. You and I haven't even talked about it. I admit I haven't done anything about it because I don't want to know. I just can't even imagine it. If it were true, I would feel so cheated. So I don't want to know."

We dropped the conversation there and busied ourselves for our next activity.

I was suddenly exhausted. I felt guilty for having lost it, for having exposed my own feelings. Not so much guilty on my parents' behalf, but on my own, that after all the time in therapy, I was still prone to an instant flare up. Equanimity, schmeck-quanimity.

Why? I asked myself. *Why do I get so aroused?*

I had come to accept, or thought I'd come to accept, that my parents were as they were and they were not going to change. I had done the inner work to let go of my anger and disappointment that they had not helped me to get to the bottom of the Kaye Wechsler story. I had come to accept it was a mystery we would never solve. I thought I had done all I could and had put it to rest.

Apparently not. In a flash, I was ready to self-combust.

———

The following spring, I traveled to Florida, this time to see my parents' new home for the first time, where they'd decided to settle for their retirement years. We hugged and kissed hello, and then with excitement brimming in their expressions, they showed me their new home. An hour later, after we had done the tour of the whole development and I'd met some of their new friends, we settled into the living room to enjoy a glass of iced tea and chat for a while before dinner.

"Well, shall we show her?" my father asked my mother with a sense of excitement.

"Yes," she said, smiling with anticipation.

My eyes widened in expectation. What could they have to show me after the complete tour of everything?

My father reached down beside his chair and lifted a briefcase onto his lap. He clicked open the lid, reached inside and handed me a sheaf of papers. Quickly, my eyes lit upon the letterhead. Bureau of Vital Statistics...State of Florida. I turned the page to find a photostat of your birth certificate, Kaye, staring me in the face.

I glanced at it, and then up at my father and mother. They looked back at me with expectation.

"It's Kaye Wechsler's birth certificate," my father said.

"Yes, I can see that," I began.

"She has a different birth date, Barb. So, she is not your sister."

Again, I experienced that sense of finality, accompanied by that same air of relief I'd noticed when he told me about his attempt to get the hospital records and learned they had been destroyed.

I looked at the birth date. Twelve days after mine.

Twelve days. Not twelve years or twelve months. Twelve days. Unexpected emotion rolls though my body like a flash flood in an arroyo. I was getting closer. When I'd started I didn't even know what year you were born, and now I've learned official records say we were born twelve days apart.

"How did you get this?" I asked my father, not mentioning that I myself had tried to get your birth certificate and had learned that in order to do so, I would need to know the names of the birth parents on record.

A smug look came over his face. "I have my ways," my father said.

I sat silently, trying to take in the implication of this new information.

"Ready for dinner?" my mother asked.

Truth is, that visit with my parents flattened me. I'd thought I had let go of ever finding you, feeling that the intensity and security of my spiritual path had resolved it all for me, allowing me to detach and accept the mystery while letting go of the suffering. But clearly, the issue had not let go of me. Every time I counted it done, something came from my parents' side which drew me back in.

First it was the visit with Aunt Margaret which had thrown my dad, and then his telling of the experience threw me.

And this latest bit, my father getting your birth certificate, really pulled me back in. He would have had to know the names of the parents on your birth certificate in order to obtain it. Thinking he was providing me with concrete proof, he was actually waving a big red flag in my face.

Twelve days younger. That's fudgeable, easily fudgeable. Twelve weeks, twelve months, twelve years, not so much. I'd had confirmation that you graduated from high school in my year. It never occurred to me to ask for your birth date, assuming it would be the same as mine.

CHAPTER 21

1985

THAT YEAR, AFTER MY PARENTS LEFT, MY LIFE TOOK A total downturn. Nothing seemed to fit me anymore. Sally and I broke up and I felt confined by my job at Children's Hospital. I responded to the malaise as I had in my early twenties--I quit my job and fled.

In the first instance, I'd traveled cross-country for three months. This time, I enrolled in a month-long writing program at Bennington College. After I returned to Cambridge refreshed and all ready for a new start, I landed an interesting job at a drug and alcohol treatment center for nuns and priests. But my time of upheaval was clearly not over. Within a year after I joined the staff, the institution shut down.

Needless to say, I was at a crossroads. I no longer had the cushion of my parents, nor a partner. I had no job and no income. As a result, I had to give up my lovely two-bedroom apartment near Fresh Pond in Cambridge and move into my friend Julie's attic.

One advantage of this change was that I began to meet

Julie's friends and acquaintances, some of whom were associated with a spiritual retreat center in Central Massachusetts. They invited me to come to one of their weekend
self-transformational workshops.

Much to my surprise, when I stepped into their workshop room, I saw the smiling face of Baba staring down at
me from a row of portraits along the wall. I had not seen
nor heard anything to do with him since I'd left the D.C.
area twelve years prior. Next to him on the wall, I noticed a
portrait of a beautiful young woman.

In one of the first exercises in the workshop we paired
up with a partner to do supported emotional release work.
My partner, a woman named Noreen, went first. Her
emotional release was grief. As she wailed and cried, I
understood the words *Baba* this and *Baba* that... *how could
you leave me* ? Talking with her later, I learned that, indeed,
her grief was about the same Baba I had met. He had died
three years earlier and she was still trying to recover from
the loss. She told me the beautiful young woman on the wall
next to his picture was his successor, Gurumayi. Noreen
explained that Baba, in the intervening years since I'd met
him, had established a number of ashrams in the U.S. She
invited me to come with her to New York in the summer to
meet Gurumayi.

In the car ride to New York, I felt timid with the group,
who, other than Noreen, I had just met. Inwardly, I was
both excited and nervous, remembering how impactful my
brief encounter with Baba twelve years earlier had been.

We arrived at the ashram a little later than planned, just

in time for the evening program. As we took our seats, the invocatory chant filled every part of my being. Although I had not heard it for twelve years, it was as if it had lived inside me just waiting to come forth again. I even remembered some of the Sanskrit lyrics. Looking around, I marveled at how the scene had changed since I'd met Baba--the crowd in the outdoor pavilion numbered at least a thousand. And every detail of the structure and setting impressed me as pristine and beautiful, including the people, who emanated an aura of being dressed in their finest, whether it was simple cotton or lavish silk, their faces filled with joy as they sang.

Gurumayi sat at the front on a throne-like chair, her graceful saffron silk-clad arm rising up in spontaneous gestures of joy as she chanted along with us. It felt as if we had come off the quotidian highway, and through some feat of time travel, had arrived in what might be heaven--a place where hordes of people dropped all earthly differences as well as their individual woes and gathered together in celebration. When the chant ended, Gurumayi welcomed the crowd and then gave a talk.

She began with, "Everyone is looking for the secret to happiness, but I will give you the secret to misery--try to please everyone."

Unlike Baba, she spoke in perfect English which had the effect of taking her message, as well as the music of her voice, straight into my heart.

At the end of the talk, people began milling toward the central aisle. Noreen asked if I would like to meet Gurumayi, a practice called darshan, which means to be in the company of the truth, as well as to greet a teacher who embodies that truth. I nervously nodded.

As the line inched forward, I watched, becoming more and more mesmerized with each step as Gurumayi greeted her devotees. With some she merely nodded or smiled, or swathed them in an embrace by her wand of peacock feathers.

When Noreen and I reached the front, we sat poised on our heels waiting respectfully for Gurumayi's attention. When it was our turn, Noreen introduced me. As Gurumayi looked into my eyes, she smiled and nodded and when Noreen was done, something in me, certainly not my conscious mind, blurted out, "I met Baba twelve years ago..." and then I heard my voice say with an astonishing conviction, "...and I'm back!"

Gurumayi threw back her head and laughed. "This must be the week for lost souls," she said to me. As I prepared to get up, I was surprised to discover I'd been clutching her hand.

I walked away, hardly aware of my own body floating off to the side and then back to my seat, in a state of joy. In the days that followed, I felt as if something had shifted, as though my brain and my heart and every perceiving aspect of myself had been rewired.

The day before I went to meet Gurumayi, I had, for the first time, turned to unconventional avenues to seek the truth about you, Kaye. I had visited a psychic. This woman, who knew nothing about me other than my name, opened our session with a little test. She wanted to see if she could pick up my information.

"For example," she explained, "if I were to talk about a Bill or a Sally..."

I smiled. *Well, not bad*, I thought. *She picked up my brother and former partner, two very active and important influences in my life.*

Then the psychic said yes, absolutely, it was true I am a twin.

I don't remember if I asked for more detailed information. It seems I often didn't in that period of time. For example, asking her to tell me what had happened to my twin. I came away from the appointment as lost as when I had gone there. I didn't see how the information she gave me was going to help.

The next day, when I met Gurumayi, I totally forgot about you. *Totally*. As if you'd been erased from my mind. Not that I forgot that you existed, nor that I had been searching for you, but suddenly it no longer mattered. I felt as if all the little empty pockets in my being got filled in, obliterating that bone-crushing, aching emptiness with which I had lived for so long.

For the next year, I became totally immersed in this spiritual path. Just about all my free time was spent in the local community of followers of Gurumayi or going to spend time with her in other locations. I meditated, I chanted, I studied Eastern scriptures, one of which was the Shiva Sutras which talked about true yoga being the managing of the modifications of the mind. I was so glad I hadn't had that lobotomy after all.

On my one year anniversary of meeting Gurumayi, I celebrated by going to New York to be with her. When I went up in the darshan line, I bowed down and put my forehead to the floor at her feet, offering my silent gratitude for all I had been given. As I did so, I heard her voice, deep and gravelly, say something about Austin. I was surprised that she might be talking to me, as I had never had a personal encounter with her since our first meeting. I sat back on my heels, looked up at her and realized she was indeed speaking to me.

Again, she said something about Austin.

"Oh, no, Gurumayi. I am from Boston, not Austin," I said.

Now we were in a normal conversation, one that I might have with any acquaintance.

"No, I thought you were someone from Austin," Gurumayi said. "You look just like her. We stayed with her on the tour. I was surprised to see her here because she is very busy."

All of a sudden, the search for you was back, hitting my brain and heart with full force. I lurched up on my knees, and in my normal, lightning-paced speaking style and great excitement, I addressed Gurumayi.

"Are you kidding, Gurumayi!?" I was later embarrassed that I'd said this to such a great being. It would be like meeting the Queen, and just as you are about to curtsy, as you put your head down in the most practiced reverential manner, she says something so personal, unexpected, revelatory and life changing to you that you forget yourself and blurt out, "Are you pulling my leg, Queenie?" The words were out before I even thought about it. And behind my exclamation came the most abbreviated, yet complete, version of the entire story....I may have a twin from whom I was separated at birth, I have been searching for her to no avail for ten years....and on through all the pertinent details.

Gurumayi was so kind. At the end of my story, she said, "I should introduce you."

And with that, it was clear my audience with her was over as she turned to greet the next person in line.

I should introduce you. What mysterious words. Introduce me to the woman from Austin? Or introduce me to you? My head was spinning again, and clearly, my one-year respite from the search had ended.

————

The New York ashram was a gathering ground for devotees from all over the world. Any time I came upon someone from Texas I would ask if I looked like anyone they knew from Austin. No one ever answered in the affirmative.

Maybe I should go to Austin, I thought. Just go to the meditation center there for a chant. Before I did that, I began to have little encounters at the ashram with people I didn't know who appeared to recognize me, but usually, we were in some situation where speaking wasn't possible-- coming out of the meditation hall in the pre-dawn, silent hours, someone who was looking at me as we broke from a program, veering towards me with a smile on their face, and then in close range, realizing I wasn't who they thought and turning in the other direction.

I began to have repeated conversations with Canadians who approached me, a perfect stranger, to tell me I looked exactly like a woman from Montreal. This became so commonplace that once when I was on a work project with a large group in the dining hall, I noticed two women at the next table, heads together, staring at me, whispering in French. I smiled.

"Montreal?" I ask.

They nodded, still staring at me. I didn't know enough French to say "I know I look like a woman from Montreal."

Some months later, the Boston center hosted a group

from Montreal to come down to have a joint work weekend. I got a call from the center's manager.

"Barbara, you have to come down here. There is a woman who is the spitting image of you. Everyone is remarking on it. The woman says she has heard that there is a woman in Boston who looks like her and she wants to meet you," she said.

As I drove to the center that afternoon, I felt strangely devoid of feeling, as if I was on the road doing ordinary errands. When I arrived at the center, I recognized the woman immediately. I had seen her in New York, although I didn't know who she was. As I approached, her husband stood off to the side, a look of amazement on his face. The woman's small daughter hid her face behind her father's leg, freaked out to see someone who looked so much like her mother.

Neither of us thought we looked even the slightest bit alike. We did a little comparative inventory of our faces-- eyes, no not really, nose, well, maybe a little bit, mouth yes. We laughed and when we heard the harmony in the sound, we laughed some more.

A *lila*, we said. It's a Sanskrit word that connotes a play of the shakti, of that force field of the world. God playing with us. Teasing us, actually.

———

Over the last ten years, God has continued to have his or her way with me, joke after joke, about twins, whether it be in my daily life or at ashrams and centers. However, these years were deeply fulfilling, and even in the soul-stretching challenges, I was happy, feeling a sense of belonging, not only to the teacher but to the community, as well. Gone was the inner isolation and loneliness.

Every time something came up about twins, I saw it as the shakti, that spiritual energy, keeping this issue alive for me, waking me up and bringing me back to the search. More and more, however, I believed finding the truth would come through my spiritual path. If all those similarities about identical twins reared apart were true, wouldn't it make perfect sense that you would be a follower of the same teacher? I believed that either I would encounter you at one of the ashram events or one of these mistaken identity incidents would eventually pan out. Or, through the practices, through divine inspiration, I would discover in myself the key to finding you.

I traveled to the home ashram in India for the first time for Christmas, 1987, thrilled and terrified about embarking on such a long journey to a totally different culture. By this time, my private psychotherapy practice afforded the freedom to take an entire month off for this pilgrimage. I traveled from Boston to LaGuardia Airport to join other devotees making the trip to Bombay. When I arrived in New York, I learned that there were mechanical difficulties in our plane and we'd have to stay overnight in New York.

Five of us made our way to the Viscount Hotel, sharing a taxi and then dinner later that evening. The group included another Barbara, a warm and lively woman from St. Louis, with whom I instantly bonded. Over dinner, I learned she would be joined at the ashram by her identical twin sister, Jean, who would be flying in from California.

My heart instantly picked up its speed. Here comes the *lila*, I thought.

"That's interesting, I said. "My middle name is Jean."

"How funny," Barbara said, "You have both of us all in one. What a

coincidence!"

"Yes, isn't it?" I said, feeling my stomach muscles contract. I was suddenly shy, not wanting to disclose the vulnerability I felt to a total stranger.

Jean arrived a week later. My heart burned all day in anticipation. When I met her, I felt like a turtle shrinking into its shell; wishing, like the little girl I'd met at the Boston ashram, that I could bury my face in some loving adult's leg. I avoided spending any time with the twins when they were together. I would though, lurk behind urns or trees, trying to surreptitiously watch them together, an activity which was both comforting and excruciating.

I couldn't look away. I never came close enough in the dining hall that they might see me and invite me to join them, but I sat close enough to study them, as if watching a movie. I watched how their gestures matched each other's as they spoke.

Sadness made a very uncomfortable home in my gut, making it hard

for me to eat. I caught myself wringing my hands at odd moments.

I still couldn't look away.

CHAPTER 22

1988

IT WAS SOMETIME AFTER THAT FIRST TRIP TO INDIA THAT I met Sharon, although we knew of each other and had in fact been living parallel lives. Or perhaps parallel serial lives.

Originally from New Hampshire, Sharon entered the Smith School of Social Work the year I graduated. She was assigned to P and PI in Chicago, just as I had been, for her second clinical placement. I first became aware of Sharon the year after I moved back to Boston, when I returned to Chicago over the Columbus Day weekend to visit my old roommate Nina.

Because it worked so well for Nina to have me share her apartment, after I'd left, she invited another Smith student to take my place. Nina told me I wouldn't be meeting Sharon during my visit because she had flown home to be with her family for the holiday weekend. The good news was that I would be able to use Sharon's room.

Two years later, a colleague in Boston put together a peer supervision group. After introductions, one of the women asked, "Are you Nina's Barbara?" It was Sharon. I learned our parallel lives had continued after Chicago. She, too, had settled in Boston. She, too, had taken a job in one of the Harvard teaching hospitals and had opened a private practice in Brookline a few blocks from mine.

We became friends, then lovers. Our lives fit together like two spoons in a drawer.

Sharon started attending programs at the local meditation center with me. Then, one weekend about a year after we'd become partners, we went to New York for a big weekend meditation retreat. It was Sharon's first. The theme of the retreat was *Prayers and Blessings.*

When the retreat opened on Saturday morning, the master of ceremonies told us Gurumayi would be going around during the meditation sessions to give *the touch*, as it was called. A murmur of delight rippled through the hall. The spiritual practice of the teacher moving amongst the meditators, giving initiation by physical touch which had been so common during Baba's time had grown exponentially. We learned that Gurumayi would initiate the right side of the room in the morning and then the left side after the lunch break.

Sharon and I decided to lessen the likelihood of distraction in meditation by choosing to sit near but not next to each other. Sharon sat on the aisle of the main section of the hall, while I put my meditation cushion two rows farther forward and across the aisle in a space large enough for only two people between the aisle and the wall. Luckily for me, I thought, as the crowd filed into the hall, the space to my left was overlooked and I ended up with plenty of room to spread out and make myself comfortable.

In the morning meditation, I descended into a feeling of flotation, a rhythmic movement of energy coursing through my body. As moments passed, in my inner world, I became aware of a sensation on my left side which slowly built into a pressure. Even as I sat straight and unmoving, I felt this pressure building, gradually forcing my posture to tilt to the right to compensate.

I started to feel agitated, in distress both physically and emotionally, unable to straighten my body, unable to find a comfortable position. Then an awareness filled me of being in the womb, enveloped in turbulence building to a pressure coming from all sides as the feeling shifted to a one of movement--undifferentiated sensation, swirling, undulating, squeezing and then release. Suddenly, I dropped into a deep calm in which there was no thought, no memory, no feeling--just stillness.

During lunch, I was very quiet, still feeling the effect of the morning meditation. Sharon asked me what was going on with me, and even though I tried, I couldn't very well articulate what the experience had been like for me.

"All I can say is, I experienced being in the womb," I said.

As I spoke, the light dawned on me that the *pressure* on my left side could have been my twin. The thought of being able to re-experience conditions in the womb came as a shock to one part of my mind, while another part took it totally in stride, accepting it without question.

As we finished lunch, we talked about the upcoming session, in which Gurumayi would be coming to our side of the room to give *the touch*. Sharon was both excited and apprehensive.

"*Prayers and Blessings*," I said. "It's pretty amazing that she chose this retreat to give *the touch* after so long a time."

"I can't believe how lucky I am to have it in my first intensive. I'm so excited!" Sharon said.

I sighed. "No matter how many times I'd experienced it, that feeling of awe and anticipation never diminished. Could you hear her going around this morning on the other side?"

"Yes, a little bit. I think I was waiting to hear something, so I didn't get into meditation very quickly. Then I started to hear this *shush-shush*, *shush-shush*."

"Yeah" I said, a hint of a swoon rising up in me. "That's it! Her peacock feathers blessing people. There's something about that sound, unlike any other in the world. I could fall into meditation just remembering it. That and the smell of the oil from the feathers."

"Well, here goes!" Sharon said as we gathered up our trays and headed for the dish room.

Back in the meditation hall, I happily settled on my cushion, wrapping my wool shawl around my shoulders, eager as a child going to bed on Christmas Eve believing that Santa wouldn't come until she was asleep. I breathed deep, turning my consciousness inside so the magic could happen. Just as when I waited for Santa, it was tempting to stay alert, to see her coming in the twilight stillness of the meditation hall. I had done my share of peeking over the years and had come to appreciate that the most intimate and transforming experiences occurred when my focus was on the inner world when the teacher arrived, rather than the outer.

As I dropped into meditation, I was aware Gurumayi had left her chair and was beginning to move, not because I saw or even heard her, but because the silent energy in the room shifted ever so slightly. I felt her progression like a soft breeze's beginning, imperceptible at first, coming into awareness when my attention was focused enough to perceive it. Her slow, steady progress through the crowd filled my body with pleasure and security. My body became a well-loved infant's, dropping out of a conscious connection to the world, totally relaxing into the safety of existence.

Sometime later, consciousness returned and I heard *"shush-shush-shush-shush."* My heart opened like a night-blooming Cereus, ready for its moment. Suddenly, a waft of that intoxicating, elixir-scented breeze followed the s*hush-shush*. Every cell of my being pulled to one pointed attention, anticipating the encounter.

Shush-shush, a little louder. *shush-shush*; a little louder. *Shush-shush*, a little louder, *shush-shush*, so close, so close and I realized she is in the row directly in front of me. *Shush-shush. Shush-shush.*

And then right beside me, on my left....*shush-shush......* *WHAT?!!!?*

My mind screamed at the realization that Gurumayi had brushed over the empty spot beside me with her peacock feathers. Although she'd now moved on to me, placing her hand on my head and blessing me with the feathers, even as I felt that cloudburst of love and beauty landing then breaking over the crown of my head, sending waves cascading down my face and over my body, I was simultaneously outraged that she had swatted the empty space.

What?!?! What is going on here? What a bunch of crap! my mind screamed as the *shush* retreated. "Why did she bring her peacock feathers down on the empty spot next to me? Didn't she know nobody was sitting there?"

I felt furious. Betrayed.

We are all being duped. Here we are, so trusting, so believing in this bond, this consciousness she embodies, that consciousness which knows everything, which is our own inner spiritual energy, that is *us*. But no, she is not that. She is a sham, a person with a bunch of peacock feathers just flailing round in the darkness ! And we, so foolish! We think just because she happens to hit us that we are being blessed! Not a difficult trick if you fill the place to the brim. No matter where you strike, you can't miss.

I boiled with uncontainable rage and disappointment, only the shock of this discovery anchoring me in my seat and preventing me from jumping up and running out of the hall shrieking. The storm continued for what seemed an interminable time until suddenly, something broke open inside me.

My left side, I thought. *My left side.*

My mind flashed to the morning meditation experience, when I'd felt that pressure of being in the womb, the sense that the meditation was telling me of the presence of my twin in utero.

My heart leapt to its knees in prayer. *Gurumayi!* it called out. *Did you swat the empty space on my left side to show me something? What? What? I can't bear it! Please, please, please help me!* My heart cried out in utter desperation.

Before my heart completely finished it's outpouring, I felt an open-palmed hand land firmly on the top of my head. Everything in me--my thoughts, my breath and maybe even my heart, just stopped in its tracks as this being, with a firm hand on my head, walked a complete circle around me, like a post hole digger, thrusting itself into the earth and making a circular incision, breaking away roots, separating the clump of soil from all that bound it, readying it for extraction. When the circle was complete, she glided away.

I fell into a deep stillness. When thought returned, it asked, did that really happen? Could that have really happened? Was my meditation experience so deep it created a vivid experience which seemed physically real?

I will never know. There is no way to check it out. Who would believe this? If I were told this, I'd believe it was a manifestation of the person's mental apparatus... real in that sense, meaningful and even life changing. But it couldn't be real in the physical sense.

I dropped trying to figure out the nature of my experience and fell again into its wonder. Once again pondering-- what is the meaning in this?

When the session ended, I slowly gathered my belongings, taking my time in leaving the hall, savoring this experience which had so filled my being. Eventually, I filed out of the hall with the crowd, looking for Sharon. When she saw me, she rushed over to me, her eyes ablaze. She pulled me off to a corner of the corridor.

"Did Gurumayi come back to you?!?!"

I was startled. "I'm not sure. It felt like it. Why do you ask?"

Sharon said, "I know I wasn't supposed to open my eyes during *the touch* but I couldn't help it. I watched as she went through the rows, I saw her do your section, and then I did close my eyes as she did our section. But then, once she had passed, and was all the way over in the center of the hall, I opened my eyes again. I watched as she finished a row, and then stepped into the central aisle. Then she lifted her head up and turned to the left, as if she was hearing something and trying to orient herself to whatever it was. A second later, she began making a beeline in that direction. I watched as she moved with obvious purpose. It looked to me like she went directly to you. Did she!!??

Tears filled my eyes. I couldn't speak.

Prayers and blessings. Indeed.

CHAPTER 23

MARCH 22, 1995

*It is amazing to me, after writing you the story of
Gurumayi and the* Prayers and Blessings *intensive that happened
six years ago, I can feel so calm and tranquil. My anxious mind
rushes out there counting up the days. "It's been nine days since I
wrote you!" My soul just smiles. "Hush," it says, "all is well."*

*Regardless of what happens, only two more days remain and
then I will either be jumping on a plane, or nothing at all will
happen and we'll figure out what to do from there.*

Actually, it is we, *Ruth and I, not* I, *who will be jumping on
the plane. She has been such a part of this tale, it escaped my attention that I haven't formally introduced her or given you any of the
background about how she came to be in my life.*

———

I like to say Ruth and I met *soul-to-soul* at our local meditation center around 1989. We took an instant liking to each
other, and solely within the context of our roles in the
center, we came to know each other better. When we

compared notes later, we deconstructed the assumptions we'd made about each other. No, I was not a suburban mom of teenaged children. No, she wasn't the innocent ingenue I'd thought her to be. The strange thing was, our connection, though deep, was truly a case of pure positive regard without context or agenda. I just thought she was a wonderful and warm person. Both of us lit up whenever we encountered each other at the center. Much later, Ruth shared an incident which made me realize something else operated outside of my awareness very early on.

Customarily, we removed our shoes upon entering the center.

Ruth told me that one time she was standing next to me in a group and I'd nonchalantly placed my stockinged foot on top of hers.

I couldn't believe it! I would never do something so bold, at least not consciously! Besides, we were both in very committed relationships. I was living with Sharon and she was engaged to Richard.

One day at a social gathering outside the center, we discovered that both Ruth and I would be in the Government Center the next day. We made plans to have lunch.

My heart raced as I entered the Mediterranean restaurant. I liked Ruth very much and I feared that actually getting to know her might ruin a good thing. First of all, I was thirteen years older than she. Other than meditation, what could we possibly have in common? I didn't know if Ruth realized that Sharon and I were in a relationship, even though we were very out in the community. I regarded her as so innocent that she may not have picked up on that.

Our conversation began awkwardly. I congratulated her on her recent engagement and asked about her wedding plans. I asked about her work as a graphic designer at a local television station. When that topic had been exhausted, I turned to her family.

"How do your parents feel about your engagement?"

"Relieved," Ruth said.

I looked up from my salad, cocking my head in question.

"Relieved?" I asked.

She nodded.

"Relieved because you are twenty-eight and not married?" I probed.

No response, so I just kept listing.

"...or because they like Richard and they weren't sure you were serious?"

No response.

"...or because he's a man?"

Whoa! What? Where in the world had that come from? How awful! Was I so nervous about her discovering I was gay and being shocked about it that I'd just blurted this out? I wanted to sink into the floor.

"Because he's a man," Ruth acknowledged.

As I looked into her eyes, time froze.

We are in trouble now, I thought.

————

This was not a happy realization.

I had been with Sharon for several years and considered myself content. It was a very comfortable relationship. We had a dog and a home and we had everything in common, from our professional backgrounds, to our social spheres, to our cars, to our clothing. We could have been Chang and

Eng--the only thing we didn't share was an organ. We even took a bath together every night.

That lunch with Ruth pulled the plug--not immediately, but very quickly. If I had known in advance that there was even a possibility, I would not have gone on that lunch date. My life was good, perfect even, but I soon learned my soul had another plan for me, and once it was revealed through my heart, there was no other choice but for me to follow.

It was painful. It obliterated all my social capital, the good opinion of my community members and my own sense of who I was, but once activated, it was so clearly a date with destiny, it overrode any aspect of the life I had been living up until that point. It felt like a test between my soul and my ego, and everything I was rested on the choice I made at that point.

In one of our earliest intimate conversations, Ruth asked me, "Do you believe we come to earth broken and spend our lives trying to become whole, or do you think we come into the world whole, life breaks us and then we spend our lives trying to put ourselves back together?"

Looking back, I believe this question, and the choice I made to be with Ruth, is what catalyzed my search for you, Kaye. I would only discover much later, that beneath the surface for each of us was what a Jungian would call a *twin complex* magnetizing us to each other.

I can't wait for you to meet her.

CHAPTER 24

FALL 1994

ABOUT SIX MONTHS AGO I BEGAN GETTING TOGETHER with my friend and colleague Olivia to study a series of videos by two renown Jungian teachers, Marion Woodman and Robert Bly.

Looking back, I wonder at what moment in our viewing, at the utterance of what words or concepts, did the fire to find you reignite in my heart. It expanded and spread, crossing the border between anxiety and urgency, erupting into my mind.

You have to find her...now!

My conscious mind reasoned back to no avail--I have tried everything. It is a dead end. I felt anger arise towards my own inner voice. It seemed really unfair to insist that I resume the journey which had no end, that I step back into the painful search only to once again smash up against that dead end. *What could be different this time*, I moaned back to that voice.

Oh, that. Yes. I could hire a private detective.

But I'd tried even that!

Early last year, I'd heard an interview on the radio with a private

detective who was describing a service he had founded which used the latest information technology to locate missing people. The way he'd described his nationwide service, it was simple, non-intrusive and best of all, inexpensive.

I called them. No problem, they'd said. They'd have one of their detectives call me back for an intake within a day or two.

"Sam Steele, here," the voice on the line said. "You called for a private investigator?"

"Yes," I said. "Thanks for getting back to me. I am trying to locate a person whom I think is my twin sister."

"You think?" he said.

"Well, it's on my birth certificate that she's my twin...or that I have a twin...but..."

"Well, then, if your birth certificate says so, I guess she's your twin," he interrupted brusquely. "How'd you lose her?"

This guy had the interviewing finesse of a jackhammer. I filled him in as best I could.

"So, you're adopted then?"

"No, I'm not," I began.

"Are your parents dead?"

"N-no, but..." I stammered.

"Then why don't you ask them where your twin is?"

Unbelievably, I continued. I told him I wanted to get information in private, that I didn't necessarily want to contact you and I hadn't asked my parents because I suspected there was something else about the story they weren't telling me.

"Your parents had something to do with it? That's illegal."

He went on about the consequences of illegal baby-swapping. This time I interrupted him.

"But it was forty years ago..."

"I don't care if it was four-hundred years ago. Illegal is illegal."

"Well, I'm not interested in prosecuting. I just want to know..."

"It's not up to you, little lady. If there's been foul play, the authorities will decide whether to press charges."

Images of my father being led away in handcuffs, ducking his head as he was put into a cruiser filled my head.

"You gotta be careful with these *locates*," he went on. "You never know what might happen. I once tracked down a woman for a man. When he found her, he doused her and her baby with kerosene and burned them alive. I think you should leave well enough alone."

Shaken, I thanked him for his call and hung up the phone, more afraid than ever.

What was the point, after all? To tear up everybody's life just to satisfy my curiosity? I swore from that day onward that I would never bring in an outside party to help me. If I couldn't find you on my own, then I would have to accept that I would never meet you.

———

Weeks later, that inner urging won out again and I called Frank Fitzpatrick.

Frank, a private investigator from Rhode Island, had been sexually molested by a priest as a child, and he'd used his skills as an investigator to track down his perpetrator, Father Porter, even though many years had lapsed, even though Porter was no longer in the priesthood and even though, as it turned out, Porter now lived in Minnesota. Frank tracked him down and brought him to justice, paving the way for countless others to come forward and tell their stories of abuse by clergy. I thought Frank Fitzpatrick might be the kind of private investigator who could understand my need to track down the truth, and also to do it with heart and some finesse.

"I don't think this will be too hard," Frank said. "It'll take maybe a month or two."

"Great," I said, when a part of me really wanted to say, "Let me think about it." *Are you kidding?* my inner voice asked. *All you've been doing about this for years is think about it.*

A month later, with no word from Frank. I feared he hadn't been able to find you. I feared he had bad news.

My mind performed exhausting flip-flops.

What will I say to Frank when he calls?

I must have a picture.

I must know where she lives and works.

I wonder what will happen if he finds her and she's not my twin?

Although I wasn't hungry, I found myself in the kitchen eating two muffins back-to-back. I don't even like muffins, but they filled the void.

Another month rolled by in which I gained ten pounds-- as though I needed more heft to keep my body on the ground. Still no word from Frank. I started to feel angry and frantic.

Maybe I should demand my money back.

I was crazed.

And then Frank called.

You still live in Jacksonville.

Your married name is Johnson. Your husband's name is Clifford.

I now have your address and phone number.

I could call your house and hear your voice!

Oh my God. What would I say?

I looked at the telephone on the table. It now had the frightening power of a nuclear reactor right there in my living room. I could key in ten little numbers and activate a chain reaction which would change my life and many others.

What an awesome responsibility I held just by having your phone number.

Part of me just wanted to dial it, to hear your voice, but that was too scary to think about. I might blow it somehow, become seized by emotion and blurt out something I didn't want to say. Or maybe the shock of hearing your voice would knock me out. I'd lose consciousness and fall over and hit my head on the table, have a brain hemorrhage and die and never meet you after all, my impulsive dialing destroying all the preparation I had put into finding you.

You're losing your grip, girl.

I looked at the piece of paper with your number.

I paced.

I stared at the paper.

I paced.

I called my friends.

I wondered if I should keep the paper in a safe deposit box in case the house burned down before it was time to call you.

I don't have a safety deposit box. Maybe I should get one.

No, I decided. Just write down the information in several places.

I'll give the information to Kathi as well, just in case.

Calm down. It's just a telephone number. You can get it again anytime.

I called information.

"Could I have the number for Clifford Johnson on Odessa Drive in Jacksonville, Florida?"

"One moment, please."

Wow! Easy! Anytime I want it. I never have to lose you again!

I can't get over how agitated I am. I thought I'd be whooping it up, all excited and relieved.

I wring my hands. I just can't help it.

That night my friend Jim came over for dinner. He'd been very interested in this whole search.

"Hell, just call her!" he said.

I started to tell him the reasons I couldn't.

"Give me the phone," he said.

"No! No! You can't. What will you say?"

Before I knew it, he was dialing.

"Hello? May I speak to the lady of the house?"

I moved in up close to Jim's face so I could hear the voice on the other end. A man. Must be Clifford. My heart picked up its beat.

"Who is this?" the man asked in an abrupt tone.

"This is John Cannon. I am calling on behalf of Proctor and Gamble. We're doing a survey on product use in the home. Would there be a better time to call?"

"No," the voice said.

Dial tone.

I was relieved and disappointed. Nevertheless, we processed *The Voice* for ten minutes.

"What did you think, Jim? Do you think that was Clifford? Did he say his name? Does he call himself Clifford or just Cliff? Did you hear any background noise? Any kids? A female voice? Can you believe it? We actually listened to her house. Think of it... in a way, we were in her house. Our ears heard what she hears every day. We...."

"I get the gist, Barb," Jim said, rolling his eyes. I knew he was teasing me but also that he'd had enough. Even good friends could only go so far.

Then, unbelievably, I got stuck. After all that waiting, I couldn't take action. In fact, I couldn't seem to take any action toward anything at all. I would wake up in the morning and not want to get out of bed. It was agony to drag myself to work. Every time I tried to goad myself into contacting you, I balked.

To my own astonishment, having the information made me depressed. And, not only did I not have the energy to reach out to you when I was depressed, I didn't want to meet you depressed. I looked like crap. My face looked shallow, my eyes were dull. I had put on weight in the last six months.

How frustrating! After all this searching and all this waiting, I wanted to postpone reaching out to you until I lost weight? Even depressed, I could recognize insanity when I saw it.

No amount of self-talk motivated me. Even Ruth started to become concerned with my lethargy.

"We have to do something," she said. Something in her saying *we* got my attention. "I think we should talk about it every day."

I had been so completely absorbed with the issue, I assumed I'd done nothing *but* talk about it, and if anything,

I thought Ruth might feel bored or overwhelmed by my hyper-focus on you. I was shocked to learn I had been withdrawn, not talking about it at all yet becoming increasingly upset. My chest ached constantly, burning as though I had been running and had over-taxed my breathing apparatus. I felt I could find release if I could just cry, but my tears were frozen. The sensation of numbness spread to my face, my cheeks heavy as if they were weighed down by sorrow. Hearing Ruth's observation helped me see what I had done my whole life--kept my feelings suppressed, invisible to others, while paralyzing myself.

I was terrified of what would happen after I reached out. What if it was too much for me to bear all by myself?

God, Kaye, this was the central issue of my life. I never felt big enough, never felt I had the capacity to gather all of me together to face something. Truth is, I needed you to face anything. I needed you in order to face meeting you. How's that for a dilemma?

As odd as that sounded, I recognized the truth of that thought. I was designed to have a second in any duel. At least for a portion of my journey. Even The Lone Ranger had his Tonto. Batman had Robin. I was supposed to have you. And instead, I was on my own trying to find you.

"Yes! That's it!" I realized. I needed a back-up.

———

"I wasn't sure you would remember me. It's has been twelve years since we've been in contact." I said.

Caroline had been my mentor in a year-long post-graduate training in family therapy.

"I remember the day you presented your family

genogram as clearly as though it were yesterday. Even though as a teacher of family therapy, I have heard literally hundreds of family histories, I remember yours in great detail."

"Really?" I asked. "What do you remember?"

I was amazed as she recounted the tale. She did, indeed, remember every detail. At the end she said, "Over the years, I've wondered about you. When I'd see members of your class, I'd ask if anyone knew what had happened to you. Getting your call today...I think this is the fastest I've ever returned a phone call!"

I told her why I was calling now; I told her that I was ready to contact you and needed to have someone as a back-up, somewhere I could go if it went badly. I wanted a trained professional who knew the story already standing by. We agreed to meet the following week so I could bring her up-to-date on what had happened in the last twelve years regarding my search.

I felt better for having taken some action and relieved that I was off the hook, at least for a week, until after I saw Caroline.

I felt nervous on the way to the appointment. Given my capacity to go numb, I worried I would lose access to what I was feeling before I got to her office. I stopped on the way to Caroline's and bought a cinnamon bun, my favorite comfort food my grandmother had always made for us. I wasn't the least bit hungry but I ate it anyway. By the time I got to Caroline's, the only thing I was focusing on was why I had eaten that cinnamon bun and how it had caused a headache in the center of my forehead. I was consumed with how bad I felt about myself for having eaten it. No feelings having to do with the search or talking to Caroline. Only worries about the cinnamon bun.

Caroline was wonderfully warm and supportive and agreed to be there for me, holding a space for me to come to should I need it. I came away feeling clear and strong, knowing it was I who must find my way to action and that no amount of talking to anyone would ever change that. No one could do it for me, and suddenly, for the first time, I didn't even wish they could.

For the next week, I felt calm. At first, I was concerned, because feeling nothing had for so long been the precursor to shutting down and sliding right into forgetfulness. But this was not the case this time. I felt I was readying myself, that it was time to jump a hurdle because I knew something useful awaited me on the other side.

It became clear that I needed to go to Jacksonville. The dates of March 23 to 26th randomly presented themselves. I spoke to Ruth about it and she agreed. We made reservations with the plan to just go and see what developed.

By the next day, this plan had evolved into simply writing you a letter. Ruth said this felt more like me, to be direct and forthcoming. Although I was concerned about so many unknowns, I felt a strong urge and I had to trust the guidance I had been asking for was showing me the way.

That night I wrote the letter, easily and effortlessly.

TRUTHFULLY, KAYE, A PART OF ME IS IN SHOCK THAT I haven't heard from you. Nine days ago I wrote to you. It feels like an eternity to me, but it is still within the range of possibility that you're on vacation or something. The one thought I am trying my best to keep at bay is that you got it and are not responding on purpose. I try to imagine myself in your shoes.

Would I respond right away?

I don't know.

Regardless, I am truly feeling like a pregnant woman whose due date has arrived and there are no signs of labor. I am miserable and just want to get this show on the road.

I just remembered that I wanted to tell you about Peter, a wonderful healer who has been instrumental in my search for you. Actually, a crisis I believe is connected to my search led me to Peter.

———

Last year, I attended a multi-day workshop with my friend and colleague, Colleen. She and I share an interest in the work of Barbara Brennan, a very talented healer who wrote the book *Hands of Light* and also founded a school to train energy healers. We were thrilled to have the opportunity to learn from Barbara directly when she came to Boston, not only through lecture and demonstrations, but also to practice what we were learning with each other.

At the end of the first session, Barbara instructed the ballroom full of students to turn to each other and select a practice partner. I turned to my right and the person next to me was in the process of turning to her right, connecting to someone else. So I turned to my left and that person had already teamed up with someone on her left. I looked around me for anyone unmatched.

No one. As I stood there alone in a sea of twos, a sudden flash flood of grief, isolation and abandonment washed over me. Sobbing, I stood frozen on the spot until a staff member came and guided me to an area where the unmatched could be claimed. As if I needed confirmation of the severity of my state, I later learned Colleen and her practice partner were some distance from me and Colleen looked up and on seeing me thought, "Oh look at that poor woman," and then, "Oh my God, it's Barb!"

I was eventually partnered with a young man who, as though from central casting, exuded a sense of disinterest in the whole situation. We decided I would be on the table first to receive healing, given my state of mind. Afterward, it was more likely I would be able to reciprocate.

I lay face up on the table and my partner put his hands on my shoulders. As I relaxed into his touch, I heard the voice of the instructor over the speaker guiding the movement of his hands on my body. I continued to let go of my distress. My mind calmed and my tears evaporated. I started to feel much better. As the session ended, I heard the voice of the instructor telling the practitioners to give the practice client time to come back to normal consciousness and then help them sit up. Once they'd reoriented to the room, the partner should offer them water and/or a listening ear.

I sat up but my practitioner was nowhere to be seen.

"Oh," I thought. "He must have gone to get me water."

I sat on my table, my legs swinging over the edge, watching the dozens of dyads, one person on the table and one standing attentively nearby, offering water or putting a hand on a shoulder, listening closely.

I waited. And waited. And waited.

My guy never came back.

I experienced a new wave of shame. Unworthiness. Unlovability. Another *lila* once again--God playing with me, giving me the recurring experience of being solitary in an ocean of pairs.

The outcome of that day was that one of the staff members gave me Peter's name as someone in the area who did the Barbara Brennan work privately.

Peter greeted me cordially and then indicated the chair in which I was to sit. He sat opposite me and without speaking, simply observed me--not in the way to which I was used, by someone looking directly at me, making eye contact. It was clear he was looking at the space around me.

Finally, he spoke.

"Where's the separation?" It was clear this question was rhetorical, not to be addressed directly by me.

"Your father hurt you."

Thus began our adventure of discovery. For the first time in my history with helpers we focused on you, on what had happened and was happening in my energetic field around this question of having a twin who was lost to me at birth.

After several months of work, Peter said to me, "You must do something. This will never go away."

And here we are.

———

Today I went for a session with Peter. After we talked about my eleventh -hour position regarding the search for you, Peter suggested I choose a Rune, a Celtic system of inspiration and divination represented by images carved into small stones. I decided to draw one for you, to see what was happening on your end. I drew Fehu reversed and turned to the guidebook for an explanation of what it meant.

There may be considerable frustrations in your life if you draw Fehu reversed, a wide range of dispossessions reaching from the trivial to the severe. You fall short in your efforts, you reach out and miss, you watch helplessly while what you've gained dwindles away...yet all this is the coming to be and passing away, and not that which abides. In dealing with the shadow side of Fehu, you have an opportunity to recognize where your true nourishment lies.

My heart felt heavy after I read the meaning of the Rune to Peter. He said it was important for me to be prepared for anything and everything, that I'd dropped a huge rock into an extremely shallow pond and many people would feel the ripples.

I have to be prepared that others, including my parents, you and your parents may be really mad at me.

That made me sad, and also angry. Peter said it was still the right thing to do.

CHAPTER 26

HERE IT IS. MARCH 23RD NO CALL, NO GO.

Last night, right before midnight, I called the airlines to cancel the tickets.

I don't know what to say. Don't even know why I am writing now. It's become a habit--something to do when there's nothing to do. I don't really know what I am feeling today. Part relief, part emptiness. It feels as if something is gone.

———

After breakfast this morning, I went out for a walk in the woods with Scout. Midway down our path, I stopped and sat on a rock in the sun. I closed my eyes and turned my face upward, breathing in the warmth, feeling as if the sun itself could absorb my exhaustion and recharge my battery.

As I took it in, I became aware of a deep longing at the core of my being, to know, to have an abiding, ongoing, unbreakable experience of the guiding force of my being, in whatever form it showed itself to me. That irrefutable, unbreakable bond.

When we came back from our walk, I laid down on the futon in my study and curled up into a fetal position. Scout whimpered until I opened up so she could arrange her body right into the curve of mine. I put my hand on her heart and started to cry...and cry and cry and cry. Deep, moaning cries. Scoutie lifted her head, and when our position wouldn't allow her access to my face, she licked my hands.

What was happening to my life?

Please, God. Guide me to clarity and guide us all to peace.

I woke an hour later. Scoutie stretched and jumped off the futon—she always knows when it's time for me to eat lunch. I stopped in the bathroom to wash my face and then went into the kitchen. As I waited for the soup to heat, I opened the freezer and ate three mouthfuls of chocolate frozen fudge yogurt right out of the carton, standing in the arctic blast from the open freezer door, hyper-aware of its sweetness, and how, for a fraction of a second, it soothed something deep in my gut. For a moment, I was afraid I wouldn't stop.

After I ate my soup and tidied up the kitchen, I sighed. It was time to get back to work.

I left the house, telling Scoutie she couldn't come with me this time, and I headed over to the office. As I waited for my printer to warm up, I noticed my own bowl of Runes on the bookcase nearby.

I reached for one.

"Okay," I asked aloud. "How is Kaye feeling today?"

Raido.

I opened the book to read:

This Rune is concerned with communication, with the attune-

ment of something which has two sides, two elements, and with the ultimate reunion that comes at the end of the journey, when what is above and what is below are united and of one mind....the Journey is toward self-healing, self-change and union. You are concerned here with nothing less than unobstructed, perfect union. But the Union of Heaven and Earth cannot be forced. On this Journey of the self toward the Self--this part of the journey cannot be shared. Raido represents the soul's journey and has within it the element of Joy, for the end is in sight. No longer burdened by what you've left behind, Heaven above you and the Earth below you unite within you and support you on your way.

A simple prayer for the soul's journey is **I will to will Thy will**.

I closed the book, my fingers folding the Rune tightly into the palm of my hand. I closed my eyes and took a deep breath. After a moment, I raised it to my lips and then placed it back on the shelf.

I sat down at the desk, ready to sort through the pile of mail and bills which had accumulated in the last ten days. After two hours, my eyes burned and my head ached. I needed a break before tackling the phone messages. I went around the corner to Au Bon Pain, which I had come to think of as *Oh, boy, pain*, the place where I always ended up when it all got to be too much.

Twenty minutes later, I returned to my desk. I picked up the phone to make a call and I heard the quick tone indicating a message had come in. I dialed the access code.

"Hello, Ms. McCollough," a deep male voice began. "This is Clifford Johnson. I am calling in response to your letter." He left two numbers, one for his office and one for home.

My hand shook so hard I could barely read the numbers

I wrote down. My heart pounded as joy and terror flew together in parallel arrows through my torso, one leaping to my heart, the other to my gut.

A voice from the void! I dialed his number and heard a message saying he was gone for the day.

My mind flipped into action, filling in so many thoughts and feelings.

Kaye must be too scared to call herself. Then my mind moved to the other end of that scale, furious that men felt that they had to be the go-betweens, the screeners for women's life experiences.

Then I remembered Jim calling and not being able talk to the woman of the house. Was Clifford the screener or was there something wrong with Kaye? Was she sick?

My heart leapt to my throat. Maybe there was something wrong and her soul had been calling to me all this time, compelling me to act. I imagined flying to her instantly. I worried that after all this time, it was too late, that she was seriously ill--or worse, dead. This was an unbearable thought. Once again, my out-of-control fears made me sick to my stomach.

Why was Clifford the middleman?

CHAPTER 27

MARCH 24, 1995

I AWAKE TO THE MUFFLED THRUM ON THE SKYLIGHT. Another day of rain, the weather conspiring with me to spend a third day in bed. I appreciate nature's kindness. My swollen eyes reject any brightness, even the limited amount of sun streaming in through the ceiling's window. I lick my lips and find them cracked and chapped, as though ravaged by fever. I close my eyes, hoping to fall back into the oblivion of sleep.

Sensing my minuscule movement, Scout, lying pressed against my side, lifts her head and licks my face.

You're dead.

Reality tries to reestablish itself in my mind, but even after three days, I can't accept the news.

"Kaye passed away, you know." I keep hearing the words and voice of that stupid woman who answered the phone.

———

When I came home from the office on Wednesday night, I

brought the phone onto the bed and sat feeling excited and anxious, taking deep breaths to calm me and to give me the courage to dial the home number Clifford had left.

A woman answered. My heart leapt into my throat.

"Kaye?" I asked.

"Who is this?" the voice snapped. "Kaye passed away, you know."

That phrase rang again and again in my ears. When I heard those words, I felt myself leaving the scene, rising through my body and out through my head. I was reminded of a film I'd seen in which the camera began with a focus on a backyard barbecue and then kept moving back and up, the perspective growing more and more distant, becoming an aerial view of the house, then the neighborhood, then the state and the country, and eventually the entire globe. Then the movement reversed and the view got closer and closer, starting in space and ending back in that same backyard. The moment simultaneously held shock and total recognition, as if on some level I'd known this was how it was going to end, that Kaye and I were not destined to meet in this lifetime. This was the script. I came back to earth, right into the reality of the telephone call, once again to hear that voice.

"Are you the one who wrote that letter?" she asked with an unforgettable twang.

I tried to speak but no sound came from my mouth.

"I better get him." she said, accentuating the *him* as though I would know who *him* was.

I waited for *him* to come to the phone. I felt humiliated and enraged by this woman. *Kaye passed away, you know.* As if I would have called up and asked to speak to someone I already knew was dead. It was the *you know* that got me.

I was shaken back to the moment when I heard a male voice on the line.

Clifford was polite. Matter of fact. I heard my voice saying appropriate condolence sounds about his loss.

"So you think you and Kaye were related?" he asked.

I stammered. "I'm not totally sure," I said. All my vocabulary had been taken up by, "Sorry for your loss." I needed to get off the phone.

"Through our mother's side," I said.

Clifford went on to tell me you died of breast cancer on November 5th.

Gram's birthday. How interesting, I thought.

After two years of remission post-diagnosis, the cancer recurred last summer and inexorably led downhill to your death four months later. Clifford told me that your father lived in the Jacksonville area and gave me his number. After that phone call, I remained in bed, with the exception of using the bathroom--and when I did, I didn't recognize the crazed-looking person peering back at me from the mirror.

———

I am not eating. I am shocked at the intensity of my grief. Although I have lost loved ones before, I've never felt so crushed. I can hardly speak. It scared me yesterday when I saw Ruth standing in the doorway around noon. I knew I must be in pretty bad shape for her to leave work in the middle of the day.

My only solace now, besides Ruth, is having the computer nearby. It seems if I can just lift my head and type, I can find you in this keyboard somehow. It's the only place I've ever really known you, and it comforts me to be talking with you again, even if you can't talk back. I am not so far gone that it seems normal to me to be writing 'since you died'. That is not language that comes trippingly off the tongue. That makes me laugh.

I swear I can feel you laughing, too, Kaye. This is so absurd.

In a way, the hardest part is that, other than Ruth, you are the only one who can be in this grief with me. Under normal circumstances, if I'd lost a sister to breast cancer, I would have lots of support. The loss would be shared, since it would be the loss of other family members and friends, as well. Although my friends are kind, it isn't real to them. Their sympathy is there, but in a way closer to how it would be if I lost my job or had a disappointing setback.

That's not totally true. Today I received two sympathy cards in the mail. One from Amy, a colleague of Ruth's. And one from Emily, a woman in our book group who lost her own sister to cancer a few years ago.

These cards mean everything to me. They make my loss real. Other than the cards, there is no ritual—no funeral, no body to view. All the pain without the particulars.

I don't want to go back out into the world and yet I know I must soon or I will go mad. To leave this bed, to leave this room and especially to leave this house is to enter into a world in which you don't, and have never, existed. Once again. a part of me has to go on, pretending I am all of me when so much of me has died. As time goes on, it seems there are smaller and smaller fragments left.

Clifford told me a little bit about you, but I want to know so much more. He told me about your funeral service in the church you and he started.

How odd. You were buried on our mother's birthday.

I find it really amazing that you started a church. I wonder what kind? Our great-grandmother started a church many years ago in a storefront. I never met her, but the family considered her a bit of an odd duck. I'd never heard of her until I started following an Eastern meditation path in the seventies. My family was freaked out that I was doing what to them appeared to be an odd thing.

I overheard my mother and grandmother talking about me. "She's just like Grandma Harkins. She was a religious nut. Always searching for God."

So I am interested in what kind of church you started. I have to say I am a little nervous that it might be a fundamentalist kind of religion. I assume people don't start new churches if they are traditional. Also, since you lived in the Bible belt, I imagine it may be more fundamentalist. If that's true, I imagine it might not have been an easy thing for you to learn you had a meditating lesbian twin. I guess we would have had some interesting territory to cover.

It makes me sick to know you just died a few months ago, after I had already contacted Frank Fitzpatrick. If only I had acted sooner. But then again, I can't imagine showing up in your life one month before you died. That would have been a terrible time to meet you and maybe very upsetting to you and to your family.

But at least I would have met you.

Oh my God! I was doing morning pages back in November, when you died.

I got out of bed and went into the study. I pulled off the shelf a stack of eight-and-a-half-by-eleven notebooks and rummaged through them until I found the entry for the day you died:

I am in deep shit.

I am angry, depressed, shut-down, enraged. I don't know what has happened to me. I felt serene and buoyant yesterday. I feel down in the gloomy dumps today.

What is the trigger? Suddenly I am furious, despairing, hopeless. I feel trapped.

What is this about? Why do I get so triggered? I feel trapped. Tied down. If I can't, you can't. I am so sad. So sad. It's how I felt growing up, feeling trapped, pulling against the odds, and the odds seem to be in my own home.

I feel this knot in my gut. I have tears in my eyes. There's a bolus of energy stuck in my chest. I am stung. I am stuck.

Where is my faith?

What does that have to do with anything?

Why am I so easily thwarted?

I was so buoyant yesterday. I was my enthusiastic, energetic self.

I meant to be somewhere else by now. That's part of my problem.

What is wrong with me? I feel woefully sluggish and unconnected and unfulfilled.

I fear exposure and dissolution.

Why am I so angry? I could ignite the rage boiling in my gut.

I have to admit, most times I feel my life has been a waste and I've served no purpose being on this planet. That's pretty discouraging. I feel I have accomplished nothing worthwhile. I have made all the wrong choices.

Chills ran down my spine. Whose experience was this? I read the entries for the day before and the day after and they sounded like my regular voice, but this day was out of the ordinary. Intense, dramatic. Were you communicating your experience to me? Was I intuiting something going on which had nothing to do with my own life?

I think about times in my life when I was erratic and emotional, when my behavior or feelings were seemingly out of proportion to what was actually happening. Could those have been times when something was going on with you, not me? Could we have had a shared emotional account from which we both could withdraw?

CHAPTER 28

GOOD MORNING, KAYE.

I've been distraught, distressed, broken open, paralyzed. I feel as if I am living between worlds and am a part of neither, like a rodent in the wall. If I make a sound, someone bangs on the wall. I fall into silence and they think I am gone.

Oh my God. I feel like Gregor Samsa from the novel The Metamorphosis.. Ever read it? He woke up one morning thinking he'd turned into a cockroach. Now I know how he felt.

That is a weird image. I wouldn't share it with anyone but you. Maybe my mind is going.

It has been five days since I heard about your death, and still the only thing that makes me feel better is writing to you each day, which is what I was doing before I heard.

It feels kind of foolish. If someone knew I was doing it, they would either make fun of me or just quietly tiptoe backward to get out of my presence.

Writing to a dead person reminds me how humiliated I felt when I learned there was no Santa Claus. Did you feel that?

Wow! Really?! What do you mean, you never believed in Santa?

Talk about ironic... no Santa, no twin sister.

Was that really you who answered me? Or was it a different part of myself? It isn't a voice exactly. It's a new stream of thought coming in and interrupting my own stream of thought. And I feel it in my belly when it happens. It just occurred to me that's what an expectant mother must feel like when the baby inside her moves. I wouldn't know, since I never had a child of my own. But that sensation in her belly is real. Even though it happens in her body, it is not her body.

I'm not sure how it happens. Sometimes I fervently call out to you and you don't seem to answer. Other times, I am having an innocuous conversation with you in my head and you interrupt me with your experience.

This actually reminds me of an experience I had in a meditation retreat a few years ago, in a room with hundreds of people. I was having some crisis in my life and needed help, and was praying silently and fervently, forcefully thrusting my plea out toward heaven. Suddenly, a deep, quiet voice interrupted.

"Stop yelling," it said. "I'm right here."

My plea instantaneously ceased and I tumbled into a deep feeling of awe. It felt as if I had been in a small cell trying to get help, only to discover there was someone--not just anyone, but a loving presence--in that tiny cell with me, someone with the power to completely remove my heartache.

The only other time I remember that kind of interruption was when someone I loved (but who was bad for me) broke up with me. I was driving along in my car, crying my eyes out, calling out to God, "Please help me!"

"This is the help," the voice said. I immediately ceased crying.

So who is that voice?

Since you died, I haven't spoken to God. It just hurt too much. But there came a point that I had to acknowledge that there is a force, a loving force with whom I interact all the time, A force that is not me. Nameless Knower, NK, *was the best name I could come up with.*

So, are you and NK one and the same? When I mentally ask a rhetorical question and something not me *answers, is that you, or NK? Or does it really matter?*

In terms of Santa Claus, as a child, I believed in him with all my heart. In fact, when I was eight, the last year I believed, Santa brought me a piano! A real, honest-to-goodness, life-sized piano, not one of those dinky little toy pianos. The REAL thing! My family didn't have much money, so I never imagined we'd ever have a piano, much as my heart yearned for one. But there it was... on Christmas morning!

I was incredulous. I told my parents I'd awakened in the night and heard all the huffing and puffing as Santa and his elves brought it into the house. I laugh now to remember that my dad spent most of Christmas day in bed with a heating pad. I still have that piano, even though it's too big for our little apartment and I never play. I wonder if I hold onto it as evidence of magic, of a time when I held such a strong belief that miraculous beings like Santa existed.

It's interesting to think about belief versus experience. I had the same experience when I stopped going to church in my late teens, when suddenly it seemed we were all just doing a more grown-up version of the Santa Claus thing. We just kept on saying and praying and living as if God were a real thing. We would read stories of proof about God's existence and about miracles in people's lives, but I never saw them in my own.

I started to experiment. It seemed my life was the same if I went to church or not, whether I prayed or not. I don't think I ever got anything I prayed for. In fact, I had a better record with Santa Claus, like hoping for a piano even knowing we were a poor family. That was about as amazing to me as the parting of the Red Sea.

But what do you think? It seems if I get really quiet and listen and then ask you a question, something comes through that feels like an answer. Maybe it's like the Ouija board. It's probably my own mind filling in the blanks, but so what? I like feeling as if we are in conversation and it's not just me hogging the airwaves.

I saw in your obituary (now that's a phrase you don't often hear!) that your mother is deceased and you have two brothers and one sister. I never thought about them before, never even questioned if you had siblings! If I had shown up at the end, just as you were dying, they would have learned you were not their biological sister right when they were losing you. How awful! I would have been so blinded by my own need, as though the relationship between you and I was the only important thing, that we were the only true siblings, that I would have caused a great pain at the time of great pain already.

Thank you, NK, for not allowing that to happen.

———

Ever since I wrote you the other day, I have been thinking about our relationship, how strange it is that I have an imaginary playmate, an imaginary sister with whom I've been corresponding every day. How is this different from my childhood relationship with Samantha the dancing doll, except this one is in writing?

So, who do I have a relationship with? Since I never *knew* you, I feel drawn to connect with people who knew you. But would their experience or perspective necessarily be accurate? Would it match your sense of yourself, or even someone else's perspective of you? I wouldn't know YOU better, I'd just know their memories, what you meant to them.

It's something, I suppose. But it's not MY experience of YOU. It occurs to me that you are what I make you up to be. That seems like a fantasy. Perhaps someone in my field would call it psychosis, that I have lost touch with reality. But what is reality, really?

Aren't we all figments of each other's imaginations?

———

As I say this to you, I realize I am still in the mode of someday, *that imagined day in the future in which we will meet and be able to check out if our perceptions are true. Then reality gives me jolt like an electric prod. That is not going to happen.*

You are gone and you are not coming back. I can't go anywhere to track you down. My physical senses will never confirm nor deny my inner experience.

What will? Is it merely a choice to believe? To make up a reality that makes me feel better?

Does it mean I've made up this story of having a twin and being separated at birth? Would I make up such a story just to feel this level of pain?

Why?

Why does my whole body ache? Why do I feel this weight on my chest? Why do I cry at the slightest provocation?

Would someone in my field call this delusion? Hysteria?

Well, I know you exist....existed. Whether you and I were born from the same womb at the same time, I do not know with certainty. I have lots of clues. I have no actual memory of that and no physical proof. So what's the deal if we're not twins? Why do I have this intimate connection to the life of a total stranger?

Please let me know if you are real, if you exist, if you are my twin. Please help me. I know you have a lot more power from where you are now, and I know you have countless beings to help you.

Please, Kaye. Please help me confirm and trust my inner knowing.

Here I've been thinking I am the supplicant, but maybe you are trying to reach me.

If so, how would I know?

———

Last night Ruth insisted that I get out of the house. She suggested the simplest of outings, going for a burrito down the block. I knew she was right, but I didn't want to go anywhere. Again I thought of Gregor. How do you put shoes on a gigantic insect? I felt rusty. My body creaked when I tried to move.

I spaced out while we were eating and was not even aware I was gone until Ruth called me back to reality. What a lousy dinner companion.

As we ate our burritos in silence, I thought of how out of it I'd been recently except when I was writing to you. Am

I going to live the life of a demented hermit, up in the attic writing letters to a dead person? Oh, so Faulknerian. Don't like that idea at all, and yet that's the only place you exist for me.

Where I now exist.

"Barb, ...Barb?"

"What?" I looked up at Ruth as I instinctively dabbed my napkin over my mouth, assuming she was trying yet again to alert me that I have forgotten the normal niceties of civilization.

"Listen to what's playing." She gestured to the air around us. *Tears in Heaven*, the song by Eric Clapton, was playing over the stereo system.

"Would you know my name if I saw you in heaven..." I heard.

As the song played, everything in my gut rose up through my chest and burned the back of my eyes. My throat closed. No more tortilla and guacamole. I bowed my head in an attempt to shield my face from the eyes around me.

"... and I know there'll be, no more tears in heaven." As tears rolled down my cheeks and onto my plate, I thought, *I don't know about heaven, but there sure are plenty of tears at the taqueria.*

Then I heard a line in the song I'd never noticed when it was popular, perhaps because it held no meaning for me at the time.

"...cause I know I just can't stay here in heaven."

Castor and Pollux. The twins. One alive and one not. Splitting time between heaven and earth, together forever in the night sky. In my meditation *and* at the taqueria.

I'm going to be okay.

CHAPTER 29

APRIL 1995

SEVERAL WEEKS LATER, INSPIRED BY EASTER AND THE
spring season of renewal, I decided to go to Florida to see
my parents and Bill and his girls. After I learned of your
death, I had considered canceling the visit because I felt
too tender to be in anyone's company, but in the end,
although my grief would be invisible there, I felt drawn
toward the comforting presence of family.

After Bill and the girls went back to California, I stayed
on for a few days with Mom and Dad. As was my custom
when I was there alone, I spent part of each day at the pool
sunbathing and reading. Since neither of my parents liked
the sun, I looked forward to these respites where I could be
on my own. However, much to my surprise, on the second
day, my father came to the pool and joined me.

Stretched out on adjacent lounge chairs, we chatted
about the weather and about happenings around the
community clubhouse. He told me he had recently taken up
tennis and had joined a men's group which played every
Thursday morning. After the game, they'd all go to McDon-

ald's for lunch. My father was always a good storyteller and I relaxed into his amusing tales about the fellows chiding each other over their Egg McMuffins.

"Oh, yeah," he said. "We have a pretty good time. But you know, Barb, I always feel as if I don't belong. It really bothers me. I guess I've felt that way my whole life and I just can't seem to shake it. I think these guys like me as much as they like each other. I think it's just me."

"That sounds pretty uncomfortable," I mumbled from under my sunhat.

I used to like it when my father confided his emotional life to me, but ever since the incident in Cambridge when he had told me about his reaction to realizing he could have been given away as a child, I'd steered clear of these kinds of discussions. I had gotten so angry that he couldn't see the very things he felt wounded about were the very ways he had wounded me and I was no longer willing to be such a supportive listener.

There was a pause. I hoped we would move on to another topic.

"I've felt as if I don't belong from the time I was a kid," he continued. "I didn't feel as if I belonged in my own family. Gus never even adopted me."

"I know, Dad. But your younger brothers and sisters adored you," I said, probably for the millionth time in my life.

"That's because they didn't know I wasn't really their brother. Don just recently found that out from Peg. Even as a grown-up, he was shocked."

"Yeah," I said. "Kathi told me how your mother told her about it when she was a teenager. One day when she was getting ready to go on vacation with us, Gramma, in a fit of jealousy I guess, told her you weren't really her brother. How mean!"

We fell into silence for a few minutes.

"You know, Dad, it's weird to me that both you and Gramma say you're not really their brother. You are biologically their half-brother. You all have the same mother. So, what your siblings found out is, not that you aren't their brother, but that you are their half-brother."

He half-snorted, half-harrumphed at my analysis.

"That's a bunch of crap, Barb" he said. "Half is the same as nothing!"

His words felt like a sharp, hot object crashing into my face.

Half is the same as nothing.

I grew quiet, glad to have the privacy of the sunhat, relieved to be on a parallel lounge chair so he couldn't see my face. I wonder what my face would have shown had I been looking at him when he'd said half is the same as nothing. I'm sure it would be a reaction very familiar to me, tension in my jaw, my eyes narrowed, an attempt to defend myself against a blow that had already reached my solar plexus. When my face is exposed, the goal instantly becomes not to show the pain in my expression, not to be vulnerable, not to be angry. Under the privacy of the sunhat, I could just feel the blow, allow the wince and feel the warmth of tears arise.

Half is the same as nothing.
Don't I know it, Dad.
Half is the same as nothing.

I couldn't stand the reverberation of his words throughout my whole body. These words have lived in my core my entire life. A perception, an inner reality, a feeling state...whatever one would call it. And my whole life had been spent trying to cover it over, using everything at my disposal to prove to myself and to others that half *was* something. That half could generate the whole. When my grandfather had ninety-eight percent of his stomach removed, they said he could live because the stomach can regenerate itself. I took heart from this evidence that if we have a part, we can eventually have the whole.

Suddenly this question became life or death for me. For twenty years, the antidote to this gaping emptiness had resided in being able to find you, Kaye. No matter what happened, I carried a sense that the other part of me existed and I would find it someday by finding you.

Now you are gone.

If half is the same as nothing, I am doomed. I felt a sense of suffocation come over me.

Half cannot be the same as nothing.

It has to be everything now.

Lying there under my sunhat, I began to wonder how I would ever find wholeness without you.

With your death, half of me had instantly dropped into oblivion. I had the image of having spent an enormous amount of energy and time unearthing a huge object of inestimable value from the depths of an ocean, and then just as it broke the surface and we were about to get it on the barge to haul in, it slipped and fell back into the depths, deeper this time, into a realm from which it can never be retrieved.

I will now live out my life split in two. Somehow, the worst of it was the invisibility and the silence around this issue in my family. Now that you are dead there will never be another reason to bring you up. You will continue to exist only in the depths of my psyche.

I felt all that I had struggled to bring to light began to slip back into darkness, where it would mold away like compost inside my cells until the hour of my death.

"So Barb. Enough about me. What's been going on in your life?"

My father's words jolted me back to the pool, to the lounge chair, to how I sweated under my sunhat. I sat up and reached for my water bottle.

"Oh, not much," I said, squirting water on my face.

"Are you happy?"

I felt my throat close and tears began to rise to my eyes. It was too late to find cover in the sunhat and too late to avoid the clenched jaw and squinted eyes. A choice point, to shove you down into the darkness by denying the cause of my tears or to allow us both to live out into the moment.

"Well, actually, Dad, it has been a very sad time for me. I recently learned Kaye Wechsler died."

I paused, for a moment wondering if I would have to explain who you were.

"Oh," he said. "You must feel as if you've lost a sister."

His response stunned me. Perhaps a question about how you'd died, or when, or even how I found out about it, would have seemed more natural to me. It made me think he'd already known this information. I wondered how.

"Yeah, I guess I do," I said.

"Would you like me to take you to see her grave?" he asked.

I looked at him with a combination of confusion and disgust. "No," I said, "I'm not the grave visiting type."

My kneejerk reaction was to reject his offer as being too

concrete. A simplistic ritual. Later, I thought his suggestion was very strange. I hadn't told him where you'd lived or died. It made me wonder if he knew where you were buried.

Again we fell into silence.

Again, that inner prompting reminding me that this was an opportunity to keep myself, if not both you and I, alive. Once again, I was at a mysterious turn in the story with my father. I was tired of this cat and mouse game and I was tired of searching. I wanted to unhook myself—not from you, Kaye, but from my father's role in this.

"Dad, I've done a lot of work over the last fifteen or so years, trying to search for the truth of this story about Kaye. As a result of what I have uncovered, I have reached some conclusions. I want to share with you what they are. I realize you live in a lot of pain because your mother died without keeping her promise to tell you who your father was. It makes me think of all that has not been said between us about this twin mystery. I don't want you to be lying on your deathbed with a heavy heart. Nor do I want to be."

"Through the many twists and turns of the story, I have concluded that I was indeed a twin and that you had a hand in giving my twin away. Although it was a painful realization to come to, I understand how it could have happened."

Stillness threw a blanket over the space between us. As it settled, I noticed my heart beat at a slower, more relaxed pace. My body felt upright and strong, as though a hand was centered on my lower back. For a moment, I felt the poise of a ski jumper who was well-prepared and ready for the descent, and my father's face was that of a rapt spectator, waiting to see what I was about to do.

"First of all, just five years before I was born, your stepfather gave away your sister Donna. At the time, he had four kids at home, a recently deceased son and a sick and grieving wife in the hospital. Not to mention he was an alcoholic. Giving the baby to the neighbors to care for appeared to be a logical thing to do. It makes sense to me that by the time I was born, the only role model you had had for what a decisive, problem-solving husband and father would do was what Gus had done. I am certain giving away one of your babies made sense to you at the time. You and Mom were teenagers with a three-year-old already and didn't need two more babies. Good grief. You didn't even need one more. Mrs. Wechsler was going to be in a bad way to learn her baby had died. It seemed a wise and compassionate decision which would alleviate stress and pain for both mothers, not to mention both fathers.

"You must have felt so overwhelmed! Here you were trying so hard to do the grown-up thing after having gotten mom pregnant when she was fifteen and leaving her behind. You did the right thing. You went back, you married her and now you were bringing her and Joyce to live with you in Florida. You probably weren't thinking about her getting pregnant again as soon as you moved in together, much less for two more babies to come along so quickly!

"I think about you and Mom when I hear stories on TV about young kids who put newborn babies in trash cans or even kill them. You didn't do any of those things, but I am sure you felt just as desperate. I am sure when the opportunity came to send one of the babies to a good home it probably seemed like a godsend to you.

"So I think you did what seemed a responsible and logical thing. You gave one of us away. And I know you couldn't have done this on your own. There must have been a doctor or a nurse helping you. And I assume Mr. Wechsler? I assume you didn't tell Mom. She was knocked unconscious before my birth so was not awake when the second baby was taken from her. You probably figured she would never know the difference.

"And I am sure you never thought there'd be a birth certificate which said I was a twin. Maybe you didn't even know Mom knew about Mrs. Wechsler and her delicate status. You certainly never bargained on the fact that she would keep the story alive by telling it to me and then I would start poking around to try find out the truth.

"I imagine this has been hell for you to have such an enormous secret that there is no way to come clean from. I mean, how could you ever tell Mom that you gave away one of her babies? Such a big mistake that, even as you matured, if you felt remorse, you could never make it right. You couldn't go back and get the other baby. Plus, in the years since, Mom has said as much about her own failure to track her down. She said she would feel so cheated she didn't want to find out the truth."

"So, Dad, I just wanted to let you know this is the story I have put together, the story I live with as the truth in the matter. Unless you tell me differently, I am going to accept this as the truth. And when you are on your deathbed you will know what I think, and you will know that I understand how it happened. And as painful as it has been for me in my life, I forgive you."

I stopped and looked at him. After a moment of silence, he shrugged his shoulders, and with no expression whatsoever on his face, looked me in the eye and said, "I don't know anything about it."

Once again, my heart sank. Although I had come to

these conclusions, a big part of me hoped my father would protest, would vehemently deny such outrageous accusations. He didn't show any emotion, no distress that the daughter he professed to love so dearly would believe such a story about him. His words of denial appeared obligatory, the carefully constructed witness stand disavowals of the obviously guilty.

Or could it be possible he was so shut down he didn't have the energy to protest? Could I be falsely accusing him? Could I have constructed this whole story out of nothing?

I thought again of Kim mistaking me for you, Kaye. I didn't make that up. I didn't make up the story of Mrs. Wechsler losing her baby, nor my birth certificate.

In the end, my father won his stonewall gamble. Without his acknowledgment, I would never know the truth, unless we exhumed your body and did DNA testing. He was sticking to his story. He was doing to me what his mother had done to him.

He will go to his deathbed without offering me release.

After a considerable pause, he said, "Barb, maybe you just made this up, maybe you just need a dramatic story."

His calmness, his slightly squinted eyes, made me think he was trying to defend with an offense. I felt as if I had been slapped. Heat rose from my belly, up through my heart and into my throat. I was angry.

"Thanks for the compliment, Dad, but I don't think I'm that creative!"

CHAPTER 30

MAY 1995

CLIFFORD CALLED TODAY.

I wrote him a detailed version of the whole story, that there was a possibility you were my twin. I enumerated all the evidence I had to support that idea--the story of my birth, the birth certificate, The Dinner Party. I ended by asking if he would allow me to see a photograph of you, either by mail or in person.

Judging by how soon his call came after I mailed the letter, he must have dialed me the minute he got it.

Well, maybe the second minute. Apparently, the first minute, he called your father. Clifford was calling to ask me to send a photograph right away because he and your father will be getting together day after tomorrow and he wanted to see a picture of me.

Meanwhile, he spent an hour telling me why this story couldn't be true.

"Kaye looked just like her daddy," Clifford said. "And that don't come from just living with someone. Hell, if that was the case, after twenty-seven years of marriage she'da looked like me."

I thought that was pretty funny and it made me warm to his style. I was not totally put off by this reasoning, as I know more than one adoptive family in which one would swear the kids looked just like the parents.

He said, though, that my voice didn't sound anything like yours. That gave me pause.

Clifford went on to tell me about you. He said you were a perfect person in every way, that you were the kind of person who could light up a room just by walking into it, and depending on your mood once you got there, you could just as easily darken it. You had an infectious giggle and he said you were a very loving mother to your adopted son.

Clifford told me you were high school sweethearts, and after graduation he went on to play ball professionally and you went to modeling school.

Well, that pretty much convinced me we couldn't be twins. I was never modeling material. But then again, with all due respect, your high school picture didn't impress me as the beauty queen type. Who knows? If, as Kim said that night she mistook me for you, that you were thinner, then maybe you could have been a model. Besides, Clifford didn't say what market you were in or if you were successful at it. Maybe you just signed up and took some modeling classes. If that's all it took, I'd be calling myself a tap dancer.

He said you had had ovarian cysts in your youth, followed by a long history of benign fibroids. I am disconcerted to hear this. My own ovarian cysts were removed when I was fifteen, having been discovered in exploratory surgery which also yielded my appendix.

Fibroids? I've had them as long as I can remember and have followed them closely my entire adult life.

I wish I had gotten the details of your medical history and treatment of fibroids as well as your decision to have a hysterectomy. All Clifford said was that you decided to have a hysterectomy because of fibroids and just two weeks later, you discovered a hard lump in your breast. He said both you and he believed the hysterectomy led to the breast cancer.

Clifford went into considerable detail about how he'd nursed you through the last year of your life. He said he had really wanted to take care of you and only called hospice in two days before you died. Both he and your son were present at the end.

Clifford said that you were a wonderful, loving person and that your funeral was the largest the church had ever seen. In fact, he said, they had received hundreds of calls a day while you were sick.

Clifford went on to tell me that he'd remarried three months after you died. Ah, yes, as they say, women mourn, men replace. His new wife Diana was someone from the church who had helped care for you in your illness. It was she who had answered the phone when I'd called, saying, 'Kaye, passed away, you know."

When Clifford learned I'm a psychotherapist, he told me he is in therapy for the first time in his life because he has just now, after six months, begun to mourn. I didn't comment, but wondered to myself how complicated it must be to have mourning set in after he has already remarried.

After we had talked awhile, we returned to the issue of me sending a picture.

"Clifford, I can understand your wanting to have a

picture, wanting to check this out, because that's exactly what I have wanted for the past twenty years. Can we exchange photos? Or better yet, I am happy to come down there at your convenience and you can see me in person and show me pictures of Kaye."

"Well, I think it would be better if you just sent us a picture first. Besides, my father-in-law is going to be here Friday and he really wants to see a picture," he said.

I paused to think about what he was saying. His urgent need couldn't wait, couldn't negotiate. Everything in me said *no, don't send a picture.*

"Clifford, it may be hard to understand, but I don't want to send a picture without having the opportunity to see Kaye's likeness, as well. I've been searching for her off and on for twenty years and I really need to see her with my own eyes. If I merely send you a picture and you don't see any likeness, that won't put it to rest for me. I will then forever wonder if I'd sent the wrong picture, or if there was a resemblance you didn't see. There would be no benefit to me to send a picture without getting one back. Is there a reason you wouldn't want to meet?"

"Well, I'd have to think about that," he said.

———

Aside from the picture issue, I was very unsettled after my conversation with Clifford. I felt an irrational jealousy, as though you had gotten the better life. I imagined you as pretty and privileged, living the glamorous life of an ex-professional ball player and model and then going on to a successful career. Somehow, it seemed as if all you'd done was much more interesting and important than what I had done with my life.

When I shared some of these feelings, my friend Olivia said "Oh, sibling rivalry." She recognized the symptoms right away. I was surprised, because I'd never felt these feelings in my relationship with my sister Joyce. Maybe the difference in our ages lessened it.

Another friend brought me out of my pity party fast by saying "Well, how lucky could she be? She got breast cancer and died by the age of forty-five!"

Nevertheless, the conversation with Clifford continued to gnaw at me. I felt unworthy to be your sister, as if Clifford and your father had the power to accept or reject me as your twin--their resistance a sign that I could not possibly measure up to you. As though being your twin was not a matter of biology, but a matter of aspiration.

I tried to talk myself down from what I recognized as irrational feelings and to expand into a perspective larger than my own. I could hardly imagine what it would be like to be in the midst of mourning a loved one and then get a call out of the blue from someone claiming to be your loved one's twin.

That is intense! I can understand the impulse to just shut down. Denial can be a sanity-preserving defense. I know it well. On the other hand, wouldn't they be curious? Wouldn't they want to follow this up? I guess they are if they are asking for my picture.

But why are they reluctant to let me see yours? Do they hold some primitive belief that by having your picture I might be able to harm you in some way?

Regardless of the reason, I was furious that they wouldn't give me a picture of you. I felt so powerless and infuriated that they'd set themselves up as the keeper of your likeness. It was like they owned you and therefore own me. I have been wracking my brain to figure out another way to get your picture.

———

It's been two months since I last wrote you. Not that I've been too busy to write. I've been in a depressed slump. Or maybe more accurately I'd say I've been numb. Too numb to take much action on anything.

I did write Clifford two more times trying to get pictures. I suggested I come to Jacksonville when I go down to Florida to see my parents.

No pictures. No response at all.

Some think I was foolish or maybe stubborn not to have sent pictures of me when they asked. Few understand why I wouldn't. After all these years of searching, I needed to see your face in order to put this to rest. I feared they would not see a resemblance--either because it wasn't there or because it was too threatening to them (I know about these psychological defenses). If they told me I look nothing like you, would I believe them? Or would I wonder if I had chosen the wrong picture, one that didn't particularly reflect the resemblance?

No. I needed to trust my own eyes, not somebody else's.

Maybe I am stubborn. Maybe I've got bullet holes in the toes of my shoes now, having shot myself in the foot. What can I say?

During those weeks though, I started to talk to you even more in my prayers, asking you to intervene with Clifford. I don't know if that means you won't or you can't or that you aren't getting my messages.

Then I started again asking you to speak to me from the other side, you know, like the vision thing. Yes, we are twins, no we aren't twins.

So far, nothing, unless you are being so indirect that I am not getting it.

CHAPTER 31

I AM SO ANGRY. FURIOUS. ACTUALLY, FURY WOULD BE A euphemism. Rage is the word I am looking for.

I just read an article in the latest New Yorker magazine. Diane saw it and called me, saying I had to read this fascinating article about twins and the whole nature versus nurture debate. The thrust of the article was that nature is winning out in the debate, that in terms of moods, behaviors and personality, we are destined to be who and how we are.

Maybe so. I'm not necessarily arguing otherwise, but wait until I tell you what a lot of the argument in this article is based upon. I am supposing that although you get my e-mails in cyber-heaven, you probably don't get the New Yorker. If you received magazines and fliers and all the other garbage that comes through earthly mail, I guess that would be hell, not heaven.

Anyway, back in the 1960's, there were these twin girls, whom the article refers to as Amy and Beth, who were surrendered for adoption. A prominent psychiatrist, a Dr. Peter Neubauer, consulted the adoption agency and advised the agency to place the twins in separate homes, saying raising twins would be an undue burden on the adoptive mother and on the twins themselves, in terms of their development, and they would be better off being placed in separate homes. At the same time, he recognized this was an ideal opportunity to study twins reared apart from birth, since all the data at that time came from retrospective studies of twins reunited in adulthood. Separating the twins from the start would serve to test a major tenet of analytical psychology, which is that our experiences in life (including those provided by our families) makes us into who we become.

So Neubauer set up a study bringing together professionals from many different disciplines to conduct this ten-year study. The real clincher was this: neither of the adoptive families were told their daughter was a twin. They were only told that their daughter was involved in an ongoing child development study and they needed to participate in testing at predetermined intervals.

The girls went to similar homes—Jewish families from upstate New York which consisted of a stay-at-home-mother, a father and a brother seven years older than the twin girl. However, Amy's family was lower middle class while Beth's was well-off. Amy's adoptive mother was insecure, overweight and socially awkward. Beth's mother was slim, youthful-appearing, stylish, poised, confident and had a cheerful disposition. In other words, Amy got a bummer of a family who saw her as a problem, while Beth got the family who doted on her and held her in high esteem.

I'm sorry. I have to read you part of this verbatim:

"Amy's problems began early and progressed in a disturbing direction. As an infant, she was tense and demanding. She sucked her thumb; she bit her nails; she clung to her blanket; she cried when left alone, she wet her bed, she was prone to nightmares and full of fears."

The article goes on to spew some psycho-babble about the cause of her problems and postulate that her life would be different if she had been raised in a home like Beth's.

However... here's where it gets interesting:

Beth's development was identical, despite being raised in the "ideal home". She sucked her thumb, bit her nails, clenched her blanket and wet her bed. As she got older, she was afraid of the dark and of being left alone.

Both girls were hypochondriacs, both became lost in role-playing and had an artificial quality in her personality. (Really? I've got to look this up. Can young children actually feign illness or over-focus on their bodies?)

And here's the piece that broke my heart--on psychological tests, each gave vent to a longing for maternal affection eerily like each other. My stomach turns at that. When researchers see evidence of longing for maternal affection... how did they differentiate that from longing for their identical twin?

I am sickened on every level reading about Amy and Beth. My own stomach curls in upon itself in a knot so tight I have to bend forward in pain. I put the article down after reading the preliminary conclusion of the author: "Were they destined to become the people they turned out to be because of some genetic predisposition toward sadness and unreality?" *He goes on to ask,* "What would psychologists have made of either girl if they did not know that she was a twin? Wouldn't they have laid the blame for the symptoms of her neurosis on the parents who raised her?"

I am consumed by the most obvious question to me: Did anyone ever, during the time of the study in the 60's, up until the New Yorker article thirty years later, ever, even for a second, wonder if the distress these little girls experienced was at all linked to being separated, and on top of that, to have nothing in their environment (i.e. their parents) reflect back to them a fundamental experience of who they are: identical twins.

I am thrust back to my experience as a little four-year-old, wringing my hands and asking if my mother was mad at me, having painful stomachaches and headaches and being admitted to Children's Hospital. Yes, I bit my nails, (still do) I wet the bed (no longer), fear the dark, thunder and lightning, of whether dogs would get fed. I think I was way more terrified than I can remember.

I wonder again when Samantha, the dancing doll, came into my life. Is it accurate that it was right after my hospitalization? Was this yet another genius-crazy *intervention? Who would have thought to give me a life-sized doll that I could strap to myself as the antidote to my hand wringing (which meant it was also the antidote to twin-loss)?*

I would give anything to be able to compare notes with you and your early childhood.

CHAPTER 32

MAY 1996

My BIRTHDAY HAS ALWAYS BEEN A CHALLENGING TIME. I have photos of me as a child scowling over a cake, about to blow out candles, with my mother hovering over me, a dark expression on her face as she loomed out of the shadows. In the candlelight, it appears the camera had caught us mid-conflict. This would not surprise me.

I feel my birthday in my stomach. It is a day I can never be loved enough, never have a celebration or gift that truly satisfies. Since 1975, after The Dinner Party, I came to understand what all those childhood photos of my birthday probably signified, how that day above all others was a day I was wired to share. But then again, maybe I was just a crazy kid who didn't like her birthday. Perhaps I've made it all up.

The first birthday after your death was even more excruciating than any other. I felt hollow. I had good friends who gathered with me to celebrate and it felt as if a lot of energy was spent trying to distract me from the pain of hearing about your death two months prior. I wanted to jump out of my skin. It took all of my energy to lasso myself in enough to bear the angst, praying the day would pass before I exploded.

A few months before the second birthday after your death, I learned my beloved teacher Marion Woodman, would be giving a *Body Soul Rhythm* workshop at Kripalu, a meditation retreat center in Western Massachusetts. It felt like the perfect opportunity to be swaddled in a safe environment, to use all that arises coincident with my birthday to go deeper into my inner experience in hopes of healing once and for all. This workshop seemed especially fortuitous, since it was Marion's work that I was doing with my friend Olivia in August of 1994 which had set off my decision to hire the detective who found you as you were dying.

Marion's *Body Soul Rhythm* approach works with body and psyche together, leading participants to experience that truth that the body holds in a way which is inaccessible to the various talking therapies. The eight-day Kripalu workshop was perfect for me because my birthday fell on the sixth day, allowing plenty of time to be settled and immersed in the environment and two days afterward to process the work itself. Having attended workshops with Marion in the past, I knew context could be important in the event that something deep erupted.

I splurged and reserved a single room on the fourth floor adjacent to Kripalu's famed healing center. In any free time, I planned to take advantage of the superb bodywork that was a signature of Kripalu itself. I was feeling nervous about my mission for this visit and wrote a letter to Marion to let her know what this week represented to me and that I would be having a birthday in the midst of the workshop.

I made the three-hour drive from Boston to Lenox, and arrived in plenty of time to get settled in my room before dinner and the opening session of the program later that evening. Although my preparations allowed me to ease into the environment, I felt apprehensive as I settled into my back jack on the floor and watched as the twenty-nine other participants arrived and joined the circle. The tingling sense throughout my body reminded me that this was no ordinary workshop for me. I wasn't sure what to expect, but my intention was to use this time to further a deep healing of my loss and to solidify my inner relationship to you. That agenda, coupled with my approaching birthday, accentuated my feeling of being alone even though I was amongst like-minded, kind and loving women. After all, they were still strangers to me. I looked around the circle before we began not sure if I was hoping to see someone I knew from Boston or hoping not to.

My unease evaporated when Marion arrived. My whole body relaxed as it remembered that any gathering with Marion held the warmth and love of the Divine feminine. It was the central theme of her work, and being in her presence enveloped us with acceptance and love. When the evening program concluded, as we all milled about in the dimly lit, tiny shoe room, I bumped into the person beside me who was bent over reaching for her shoes. I looked up to apologize for knocking into her.

"Caroline!" I gasped. "Oh my God! I can't believe you're here!"

I hadn't seen Caroline since the day I'd gone to see her and she'd helped me to make the decision to write to you. We had talked on the phone about the outcome, but we had not been in touch in the intervening two years. My heart instantly eased, knowing Caroline would be present for anything that came up for me in the week ahead.

Marion's *Body Soul Rhythm* features mask-making as a means of bringing to consciousness energies which exist in our psyches outside of our awareness. Once these energies, or archetypes, are put into the physical form of a mask, we can interact with them and come to understand how they operate in our lives. Although each of us starts with something in mind, the actual process takes on a life of its own as we go deeper into ourselves through lectures, exercises and the process of making the masks. As we proceed, the masks come to look different from what we consciously intended (like all art!) and when we wear them and interact with others, we experience parts of ourselves seeking expression.

As the assistants went around distributing the materials, they emphasized the importance of conserving the materials so we would have enough to go around. I felt a pang in my gut, because it was essential for me to make two masks, which meant I'd be using double the amount allotted to me. I could feel energy flow into my solar plexus, readying me for defense should my mission be thwarted. I calmed when we formed into pairs to cast each other's faces and Caroline took her place beside me. There would be no need to explain my need for a double mask.

We settled into the work of applying wet plaster strips on each other's faces. I went first, and after we made one mask, we put it aside to dry and repeated the process to create the second. From the moment I saw them lying side-by-side, it felt totally natural to have two faces, and yet it was eerie to see these two white plaster faces in my own likeness. With their eyes and mouths closed, they were reminders of the ultimate blindness and muteness of death.

That evening, we gathered for an arts and crafts session, a warm-up to prepare us energetically for the following day's mask decorating. Much to my surprise, my free-form drawing took the shape of a mushroom cloud, bronze and cream central images surrounded by orange and red swirls.

The following day we began decorating the masks. I wanted to experience a second face identical to my own and planned to decorate them exactly alike, but as the work proceeded, they became decidedly different. First of all, it was clear that the point of making the masks was so we could actually wear them later in the week, so I needed to figure out a way to wear two masks at once. To that end, I needed to cut out the eyes and mouth of at least one of the masks so I could move about the room. The second mask, which I had designated as you, Kaye, I did not want to cut out the eyes and mouth--seeing the face in repose captured for me your presence as well as your absence through death. So from that moment alone, the masks became different.

At the beginning of the decorating session, we walked meditatively around the tables of art supplies, allowing our unconscious to select the materials. I was immediately drawn to a pile of white feathers, the number thirteen and then to three red feathers. When it came to paint, I chose bronze and cream, which were reminiscent of the colors from my drawing the night before. I mixed them together to create the overall skin tone of both masks. In addition, I chose accent colors of orange and red.

I decorated your mask first. I arranged ten of the white feathers from the top down around the left side curve of your face. As I worked, it reminded me of my mother's love of owls and also of White Buffalo Woman. I painted an orange and red flower on the cheek and the thought *radiation burn* came to my mind. To finish, I added one red feather above the brow. In the end, you looked like a sleeping 1920's flapper!

On the second mask, the one that would be on my face, the remaining three white feathers made a beard, surprising me that this mask was male. The remaining two red feathers splayed across his brow and on his cheeks. With the orange and red paint, I drew cicatrices, those parallel lines often seen in aboriginal males, on his upper cheeks, right under each eye.

I stepped back and looked at my creation. What the heck was this? I could see it was not what I thought I would be creating. It looked like an old couple. He looked either Native American or Asian and she looked Caucasian. Something about him reminded me of Pappap, my maternal grandfather. I knew if he had a voice it would be gruff and he would be a man of few words. She, on the other hand, was inscrutable. With nothing cut-out, her eyes could be construed as closed or downcast. I felt unsettled, not knowing if she was mute and blind or simply demure.

Now, in order to prepare them for the "Cocktail Party," the evening session when we would each enter the room in costume and in mask, representing ourselves as the energy we had put into our creations, I had to join my two masks together so I could wear them as one. I drilled holes on the left side of the masculine face and the right side of the feminine and then lashed them together with fishing wire. This way I could wear the mask with two faces side by side, with only the "male" having the ability to see or speak.

I stood over the table staring into this creation. What is in this face, these faces? I set out to make them you and me... the shape is like us... but who else are they?

CHAPTER 33

MAY 21, 1996

THE NEXT DAY, MY BIRTHDAY, I AM AWAKENED IN THE wee hours by a disturbing dream:

It is twilight on New Year's Eve. I am in Brookline Village where I live with Ruth. We are walking across the street, which is a bridge, leading into the heart of the village, through stopped traffic. We carry a bag with two bottles of grape juice, one white and one red. We're talking about what we want to do for New Year's Eve. I say I don't want to go to Allison's like we have in the past because we'll just sit around waiting for the New Year to turn and that was too boring for me.

I look up and see we are passing in front of my friend Olivia's car. She is on her way to see me. Since the traffic is stopped anyway, she gets out of the car and joins us on the curb. I tell Ruth to pour her some red grape juice.

Olivia says, "Have you heard this?! It's outrageous!" She's referring to news that's on the radio and in the paper she was reading behind the wheel. It's apparently the reason for all the traffic and for people taking to the streets.

Ruth and I don't know to what she's referring. She says Richard Nixon is testifying and we should especially look at the June 15th testimony, which is five-hundred pages long.

In his testimony, he said he can't be held responsible for what his hands did. He says this with a lascivious kind of chuckle which makes me feel uncomfortable, as if he's referring to something sexual. But it could be about finances, like having his hand in the till.

I can't go back to sleep. I ache in my ovaries, especially the right one.

I pay attention to dreams, an essential tool in both my professional and personal work, and never more closely than when I am in a Jungian-centered world, such as being in the midst of a *Body Soul Rhythm* week with Marion. Inherent in many schools of dreamwork is the idea that the unconscious is sending us a message and, by definition, the meaning is rarely obvious. Another way of thinking about a dream is that it is a snapshot of the conscious situation, taken from the vantage point of the unconscious.

I started to play around with pieces of the dream to see if it would release something into my consciousness.

New Year's Eve. Makes sense, I am here at Kripalu on the cusp of letting go of the old and beginning anew.

Olivia...of course, she is my task companion. We have a commitment to each other around fulfilling our life's work. In the dream she is coming to me with important news she wants to make sure I know about. In fact, she calls the dream situation outrageous.

The strongest feeling in the dream was in what Olivia

tells us of the Nixon testimony. My association to Nixon is when he was forced to resign from the presidency in the face of his deceit and his attempts to cover up his crime. Five hundred pages in which he says he is not responsible for what his hands do--in other words, for his own actions.

I searched for clues for unraveling the dream in what was happening in my life when Nixon resigned. I was on that cross-country trip after I had left Frank. The news reported that Nixon was expected to officially resign that day and as we traveled all through Wyoming, we stopped several times hoping to catch the live broadcast of this historical event. And yes, people were in an uproar, metaphorically taking to the streets. We heard his speech in a bar in the tiny town of Ten Sleep, Wyoming. But that was August. What is it about June 15th?

June 15th. About three weeks hence. I cast about searching for a calendar but can't find one. I try to go back to sleep but can't stop thinking about June 15th.

Aha! Someone will be on duty at the front desk.

"Can you tell me what June 15th is? What day of the week?" I ask the man all-but-asleep behind the counter.

He looks at me for a long moment without speaking, then his eyes fall beneath the surface of the counter right in front of him.

"It's a Sunday," he says.

"Thanks," I say, and turn to go.

"Father's Day," I hear him say.

Oh my God. Could my dream be telling me "Tricky Dick", a deceitful man who tried to cover-up his crimes, is a symbol for my father? Not to mention, my father looks a lot like Nixon.

———

As it turned out, the cocktail party in which we would be wearing our masks occurred the evening of my birthday. It was set up as a party, at which we each arrived in costume, wearing our masks and interacting with Marion and her staff and each other only as the energies in the mask.

From the moment I put on my double mask, I hated wearing it. As I mingled about the party interacting with others, I became frustrated. It annoyed me when people interacted with the "female" mask and not the one on my face. As the evening wore on, I felt like the male in an elderly couple and I was resentful of the complete depen-dence of the female upon me. She couldn't talk or see or relate to others, so I had to do all of that on her behalf. She was merely a silent, ever-present being. Nothing to excite, nothing to offend. We (my male mask and the attached female) couldn't relate at all to each other because we were lashed together both facing forward.

As the evening wore on, I became increasingly uncom-fortable and eventually downright anxious. I wanted to take the mask off, which was against the rules. I needed to find a way to let our hostess Marion know of my distress without breaking out of the mask. I approached her and we chatted, and then I said to her, "We are having trouble. Are you a couple's therapist? Because we need to separate." She, in her role, essentially told me to hold on and we'll see, letting me know I should not remove my mask. A while later, the music started to slow and one of the assis-tants directed us in removing the masks. Just as I'd taken mine off, someone protested that they weren't ready to remove the mask, so the staff member assented and said

"Okay, put your masks back on and we'll go for one more song."

No way! I thought. *I am not going to put that F-ing mask on again.*

I found a corner and plopped down on a pile of pillows just as the next song, Pachelbel's Canon, started to play. That was the last moment I was conscious.

A screaming, high pitched shriek brought me back to consciousness. Even though it seemed I was observing it from afar, I recognized it as coming from my own body. It was the shrill sound of a baby's distress cry. When I fully came to, I was lying on the ground looking up at a circle of sweet faces peering down at me. Marion had her arm around my shoulder and was patting my hand and making soothing noises. When she saw my eyes were open, she said, "Let's go to your room."

We both lay down side-by-side on the bed as she softly talked to me. She told me she was aware when I approached her about wanting "couple's therapy" that there was trouble brewing and she knew something would erupt when I took off the mask. She had intended to be nearby when I removed it but the mix up over the music and the resumption of the activity meant she wasn't close to me when I took off the mask.

I don't remember all that was said. We lay on that bed for what seemed a very long time. I remember my legs were trembling intensely, as if I was having a seizure. She calmed me with her soft voice and gentle pats. When I had returned to a nearly normal state of mind, she said we needed to think about what to do with the mask. One option was that we could bury it on the property the following day. She wanted me to think about it and said she would come back to my room at 8 a.m. the next morning to hear my answer.

I couldn't sleep. I knew I couldn't bury the mask. Just the idea of that made me gasp for breath as though I were being smothered.

I want to separate them, I decided.

I spent the night planning out a ritual of separation.

Our workshop was in the chapel of Kripalu and there was an altar in the room which would serve perfectly. First, I thought of people in the workshop who could play a role signifying what I wanted to communicate.

-Caroline, of course!

-Anna: one of the participants from the mid-west who was a judge in real life and an extremely loving and compassionate woman.

-Margo: who had told me two poignant stories about her life. The first was that her mother as a small child had been brutally ripped from her family of origin in an impoverished country and brought to the United States., where it was believed she would fare better, but it created emotional sorrow for the reminder of her life.

The second story was that she had grown sons, one of whom was about to marry. Margo took very seriously what family meant and wanted to welcome her new daughter-in-law by giving her a significant gift. She was well-off and could have afforded to buy her daughter-in-law-to-be fine jewelry that would have been treasured. However, she wanted to make a sacrifice of something precious to HER. She'd chosen a diamond and emerald bracelet her husband had given her as an engagement present, which was one of her favorite pieces of jewelry.

-Marion and her husband Ross...

———

As promised, Marion arrived at my door at 8 a.m. I told her my plan, which she wholeheartedly supported. We decided we would do the ritual in the seminar room at the altar at the end of the morning program. Those who wanted to stay to witness it could, and those who didn't want to, could go on to lunch.

At the end of the morning lecture, we took our places. I had spoken to the *handmaidens*, who were happy to participate as witnesses at the altar. I placed the conjoined mask on the altar before me, along with the wire cutters.

"Holy Sophia," I began, "Goddess of Wisdom, we invoke your presence at this ceremony of dissolution and reunion. We gather here to honor the twin souls of Barbara Jean and Brenda Kaye, who began as one in order to become two. By your hand, we release them from the firmly-tied strands which have created bondage rather than bonding. We free them to find true eternal connection in spirit, allowing each soul to complete its separate journey back to Oneness with the Divine.

"We welcome the presence of wise witness in the form of

Caroline--sister of steadfastness, of presence, of perpetual witness to the unfolding story.

Anna--sister of incisiveness embodied in compassion.

Margo--sister of transformational grief, midwife to the healing of brutal disconnection.

Marion and Ross--templates for the wisdom couple, of loving and enlightened union, representatives of the Divine Parents, consciously witnessing all while mirroring the soul of the Divine Child.

"May this ceremony be a prayer for the healing and freeing in body, mind and spirit of Barbara and Kaye, of Ruth, of Harriet and Bill, of Bill and Joyce, of David and Ruth Wechsler, of Clifford and his son and of all beings for whom this story resonates."

Through tears, I picked up the wire cutters and addressed the two masks lying before me on a sacred cloth on the altar.

"What Sophia has designed to find its wholeness in dividing, let it be..."

I started to tremble. I didn't know if I could actually sever the masks. It felt no easier than if I'd buried the masks. After a lifetime of searching, holding, wanting, needing, it was terrifying to take the action of cutting the line.

I have to do this. I have to get beyond this.

I moved to cut the fishing line binding the masks together. It wouldn't budge. I had bound them tightly so they could never be separated again. I could hardly wedge the nose of the clippers between the mask and the fishing line.

I struggled as the others waited. As I trembled and sobbed, it took everything within me to continue. I looked up to see everyone at the altar was in tears, as well.

I continued, snipping each of the dozen threads one-by-one, losing strength with each clip. Just when doubt began to creep back in, a beautiful sound filled the transept--a soft, lyrical female voice singing words I couldn't discern.

At first, I thought it was an angel, but it was Jean, one of the program participants who, unbeknownst to me, had stayed behind to witness the ceremony from a distance. She was inspired to offer her song in that moment, releasing in me a newfound strength. Effortlessly, the last threads gave way and the masks came apart.

I closed my eyes in reverence as Jean finished her song. Then I took the cymbals and as I rang them, I repeated,

"What Sophia has designed to find its wholeness in dividing, let it be."

I picked up the separated masks, one in each hand, and turned them to face each other for the first time.

"What God has drawn together to reflect similarity in difference, let it be."

I placed the masks side-by-side on the altar and once again rang the cymbals.

"May the divine forces of fission and fusion be forever embodied in the soul.

"May this ceremony be an offering for the healing of all human-induced mutations of consciousness that have been toxic to individual souls and to the soul of Mother Earth.

"May we all surrender to the natural healing direction always promised by you, Holy Sophia. In your name we offer these prayers."

I closed my eyes and bowed my head. Through my breath, an enormous peace filled my body and my mind, while love filled my heart.

CHAPTER 34

JUNE 1996

I RETURNED HOME FROM KRIPALU AND IMMEDIATELY realized the significance of June 15th. My parents and grandmother were coming for a visit which would span Father's Day.

They arrived earlier than expected and I wasn't ready for them. I'd meant to remove the Kripalu masks from the bookshelf in the dining room. Not that they would notice or comment. They rarely did. The photograph of me I'd Photoshopped to create an identical me by my side had sat on the piano for years. It would be impossible for them not to have seen it, but they had never commented.

Nevertheless, I'd wanted to put the masks safely away in my study before the family arrived, but the doorbell rang long before I'd gotten to tidying the dining room and I didn't notice the masks were still there until dinner.

In order to accommodate everyone at the small drop-leaf table, we'd brought all the available chairs to the dining room. When we were finished eating, my father attempted to push the small rocking chair he was seated in away from the table. It wasn't a scootable kind of chair and he clumsily bumped into the bookshelf.

"Oh. Oh!" he said, as he heard something fall to the floor. As he attempted to move around so he could retrieve the item, I heard a crunch. I looked down to see the feminine mask, the one which had represented Kaye, under the runner of his rocker. I jumped up and took it from him, as well as the other mask still on the bookshelf.

"Oh, sorry! My eyesight..." he said as I gathered the items. "What is that, anyway?"

"It's an art project," I mumbled under my breath. "I'm just going to take it into my study."

One of the purposes of this visit was that my father had been having trouble with his eyesight and he'd had a hard time finding good treatment in Florida. I had suggested that I make an appointment for a second opinion at the Massachusetts Eye and Ear Infirmary in Boston, which had a stellar international reputation.

On the morning of the appointment, I opened my eyes to see my father's head on the floor. At first, I thought it was a dream, then realized that it was my very much alive father who had climbed up the spiral staircase to our bedroom and had stopped when his head was visible enough to see into the room. I instantly knew what was happening.

"It's too early, Dad. You can go back to bed. I have the alarm set."

"Oh. Okay, then" He started to back down the stairs.

My father was so much like a child. I knew that the reason he had crawled up the stairs was that I was taking him to his appointment, just me and him. And he was excited about that. I was sure he also had some jitters about the actual appointment, but I knew my father was always eager to have me all to himself. He always said at the end of any private time, "You really give me a lift, Barb."

We went to the doctor's appointment and afterward, I suggested we go for breakfast. His eyes lit up as I knew they would. We settled into the booth at Brigham's and ordered our bacon and eggs, and then Dad cradled his cup of coffee in both hands, his signature gesture when something was on his mind that he wanted to discuss with me.

I tried to open a space for him to talk into. "So, how are things going, Dad?"

"Pretty good," he said. "We were just back in Pennsylvania for a month or so. Your mom wanted to help your gram clear out some things and get herself organized. I tackled the basement while they cleaned upstairs. Whoo boy-- lotta junk in that basement!"

"God, I can imagine! That was nice of you to take that project on!" I said.

"Well, I'm not so sure about that," he said.

I looked at him quizzically.

"I found a box of stuff from your Uncle Rich. You probably don't remember him. He died when you were really little."

"I don't remember, but I know he drowned when I was two," I said.

"Well there was a box of his stuff they returned when he died and I sorted through it. Probably shouldn't have."

He sipped his coffee as I waited for him to go on.

"I found some letters from Gram. She was talking about me. I think you know that when your mom got pregnant and I went to join the Navy, your Gram contacted my commanding officer and made me come back and marry her?"

I felt my stomach give way underneath me. Another surprise, another little toxic secret parsed out. I hadn't known this, and it instantly made me sad for both of them. After all these years and all this uncovering, it hurt to hear a piece of the story that was foundational to our entire lives together. It meant none of us, including my parents, would ever know if they would have married eventually out of love. I knew it didn't necessarily mean they would have stayed together. They could have married for respectability and then split up for good. They were not forced to have me or Bill.

"No, Dad, I didn't know that," I said.

"Well, anyway, in this letter, she was complaining to your Uncle Rich that I was a no good son of a bitch." He broke off and looked down at his coffee. "I don't know why it upset me so much. I understand she was mad. Still, it was so hard to see that."

"Did you tell her you'd found the letter and what you read?" I asked.

"Are you kidding!? Of course not!"

I did understand. Fifty years of being an attentive, dutiful son-in-law

had done nothing to change her mind. In this family it was *once a grudge, always a grudge, no matter what*. Bringing it up to be cleared would most likely only create an occasion for re-injury.

"Ya know, Barb, it's my own fault. I shouldn't have read the letter. I suppose it's normal for a mother not to like her son-in-law."

This made me remember that my grandparents had always referred to their sons and daughters-in-law as the *outlaws.* A joke that was never really a joke. I thought of Margo.

"It may be normal, but it's not universal," I said. "I just met a woman at a workshop who really impressed me. Her son was getting ready to marry and she wanted to give her future daughter-in-law a meaningful gift to make her really feel as if she was a part of the family. She knew making a true relationship with his intended was as much a gift to her son as to his bride-to-be. She is a wealthy woman and could have bought a beautiful piece of jewelry, but she wanted it to be a sacrifice, something personal that she treasured. So she gave her the emerald and diamond bracelet her husband had given her for their first anniversary."

"Wow!" he said.

"Yeah, pretty amazing. Makes me sad for you and angry at Gram, that she couldn't change, couldn't forgive despite all the ways that you have been a wonderful son-in-law to her. Hey, look at it this way, you gave her three wonderful grandkids, so who cares what she thinks?" We shared a little chuckle and the waitress brought the check.

As my father opened his wallet, he winked at me and said, "Ever see my kids?"

He held out the photo section of his wallet and there were the two pictures that had been in there since I was around eight years old. One was a picture of the three of us kids, sitting in a row by height and age on the piano bench... Joyce, then me, then Bill. We lived in Arkansas, so I must have been in the fourth grade. The second picture is a head shot of me alone, probably in the fifth or sixth grade, which always embarrassed me. My mother never got up with us in the morning before school and I wanted to do something special with my hair for the school pictures that were going to be taken that day. I thought I'd made myself look really glamorous like my Aunt Peggy who worked at the bank. I had put my hair up in what I thought was a French Twist like hers, but the photo showed bobby pins spilling out in all directions as they tried to capture all those bits of hair that were way too short for such a hairdo. My father had carried that picture in his wallet for the past forty-some years. I never knew why. I'd never asked him. And why was I the only single one? Whenever he met someone new, he would ask, "Wanna see my kids?" It was hilarious, yet strange.

I had forgotten about the picture and hadn't seen him pull this gag for many years. I started laughing, as it had always made me do. As I wiped away the tears of laughter, I said to him, "If we go out to dinner, you gotta show this to Ruth. It's so funny!"

———

Later that night, my parents, my grandmother, Ruth and I went out to dinner at a family-style Italian restaurant. It was great fun sharing bowls of pasta and sauce and ensalada, topping it all off with tiramisu. We ate ourselves overfull. As we finished and the bill was presented, my father reached for it and got out his wallet.

"Hey Ruth," my father asked, "Wanna see my kids?"

My father extended the wallet to Ruth. She took it and looked at it, smiling. The rest of us laughed as she handed the wallet back to my father.

He took the photo of me out of its sleeve and extended it to Ruth. "Would you like to have this?"

My heart exploded. Silently, I was freaking out! NO!

You can't take it out of your wallet! What if it's been your lucky charm all these years? I could hardly breathe.

I heard my mother say, "No, Bill. We can give it to her after you're cremated."

But the deed was done. My heart was broken and broken open in the same moment. I was witnessing a solemn, meaningful exchange from my father to Ruth. He was demonstrating that he'd understood the story I had told him that morning, and he was giving to her what was as precious to him as an emerald and diamond bracelet--the photo of me he'd carried in his wallet for forty years. I was both touched and distraught.

My daddy had given me away.

CHAPTER 35

EARLY SUMMER 1998

"HI BILL, WHAT'S UP?" I ASKED WHEN I HEARD MY brother's voice on the phone.

"I'm calling to tell you something you are not going to be happy about."

"Okay...now you've got my attention..."

"As you know, Mom was out to visit..." he said.

"Yes, I know. Wasn't she flying back to Florida today? Is something wrong?"

"Yes. She left this morning. But last night we were talking about my writing and I mentioned that you're writing a memoir about your twin story."

He was right. I was not happy to hear this because I had specifically asked him to not mention what I was writing about to my parents. I had been reluctant to even mention it to Bill, but I had recently read the chapter about interviewing my father at a program at the Cambridge Public Library. This was a first for me, and I was very excited it had gone so well. I'd wanted to share it with my writer sibling.

"I'm really sorry, Barb." he said. "I wasn't going to tell you, but knowing Mom, she won't tell you she knows but she'll make you pay in some way."

"What happened?" I asked.

"When I told her you were writing about the twin story she freaked out. She said, 'How could she think I would give up a child?' I interrupted her and said, 'Maybe that's not what Barb is saying.' I said that because I knew you had concluded Dad had something to do with giving away the twin and he'd kept it secret from Mom. But in her ire, Mom asked, 'Well, what else could she be saying?' Then she suddenly stopped. Her face went cold and she started to cry. She got up and left the room, and this morning she didn't say anything about it when I took her to the airport."

I was mad at Bill for doing this, but I was really grateful he had 'fessed up. He was right. My mother would never say a word to me. She would wait until an opportune time to blindside me. Much better to be forewarned.

———

Three days later, I received a call from my mother.

"Hi, Mom! How was your trip?"

"It was great. I loved seeing Bill and the girls. It was hard to leave."

"I'll bet," I said.

"But there is something else I want to talk to you about," she said.

Oh, oh. Here it comes...and so soon, I thought.

"Your father and I are splitting up."

She went on to say she had returned to Florida from

California and two days later, my father had said he wanted a separation, that he had not been happy for a long time, and while she was gone he had taken up with another woman.

There was something eerily calm in her presentation. It was hard for me to believe that after fifty-two years of marriage it could be dissolved so quickly. I don't know if she was in shock, or if, in fact, a part of her was relieved.

In the ensuing months, my mother seemed at peace. She was living alone for the first time in her life, she was getting out socially and in a sense was really blossoming. My father, on the other hand, took up smoking and drinking and his health began to fail.

Within four months of the separation, my father had to have heart bypass surgery. My mother was worried about how to manage this event now that the relationship was on rough terrain. She was afraid she'd encounter my father's new girlfriend at the hospital. Of the three of us kids, I was the least close to my mother, and yet I was the only one uniquely qualified to handle the situation, having had a lot of experience with families in hospitals. Plus, being a couple's psychotherapist, I was definitely pushed to the front of the line.

"You do it, Barb."

My father was scheduled for surgery at seven. I wanted to see him before he received anesthesia, so my mother and I arrived at six a.m. On the way to the hospital, my mother talked non-stop about how my father never took care of his health, how he'd smoked for so much of his life. Even though it had nothing to do with his current dilemma, she went on about how he had not treated his glaucoma properly when it was first detected and that's why he couldn't see well today. I knew what was really going on was she was nervous about whether she was going to run into my father's alleged girlfriend. Truth was, I was nervous about that, too.

When we arrived, my mother opted to wait in the main lobby while I went up to see my father. When I walked in, he was alone, arguing with the nurse about how long it had been before they answered his call bell.

As the nurse swept past me on her way out of the room, she hissed in my direction, "Your father is not a nice man."

"Hi, Dad. How are you doing?" I asked as I took his non-IV'd hand. He grumbled something in return as he fussed with something pinned to his hospital gown.

"Just wanted to give you a hug and wish you well with the surgery," I said as I patted his hand. "They are coming in with the sedative, so you'll feel more relaxed in just a few minutes."

Where was the alleged girlfriend? I wondered.

"Mom and I are here, and we'll be waiting in the lounge while you're in surgery." He made a harrumphing noise and closed his eyes.

"Here, let's sit over by the window," I said to my mother as we carried our cafeteria trays from the cashier stand.

Once we were settled, I started making small talk about my father's surgery, when he might be out of the recovery room and when we might be able to see him.

My mother said little in response. We ate our respective breakfasts in silence until she abruptly started talking about her visit to see Bill.

"I was upset when he told me you were writing about

the twin story. I couldn't believe you were still thinking about that after all this time. That you would think I would ever give away a child. I was crying and ranting about that when Bill said, 'Maybe Barb's not saying that...'"

She paused as she buttered her toast. I couldn't help noticing she was doing it the way her father always had, with extreme concentration and with quick little back and forth motions with the blade of the knife that made it look as if she was gently slapping the bread into submission.

"When Bill said that, I started to say, 'Well what else could she be saying?!' Then something just happened inside me—as if a curtain was lifting so I could see something new. Have you ever had that happen? And I realized, clear as day, he had been betraying me for fifty-two years."

My mother paused, putting her bread and knife down, looking away from me as she smoothed the napkin on her lap. Knowing from Bill's version of the conversation that she had become more upset after she'd said, "What else could she be saying?' I wanted to prod her. I wanted to know what unfolded with *He had been betraying me for fifty-two years*

But I held back, quelling my clinical investigator's instincts for a change, recognizing that my mother had entered a place inside herself which was really none of my business. She was not confessing to me, nor was she asking for my assistance. Much as I wanted to know, it was hers to tell or not tell.

After some time, she went on.

"I saw that it was true. Your father had known about the twin and had something to do with it, although I didn't know what. And he has kept that knowledge from me for fifty years. I don't know how I knew in that moment. I just did. I didn't want to tell Bill what I'd seen. I didn't want to change his opinion of his father. I just broke down. I felt bad for Bill. He didn't know what was going on. The next morning I came home."

As my mother finished her coffee, I sat in a different part of myself. Like her, I would be hard-pressed to describe it. The closest I can come is to say I felt as if, for the first time in my life, I had a mother. She was fully there, she was in touch with her own emotions and she seemed present to the importance her story would have on me.

For the next several hours, as we waited for my father to come out of heart surgery, we actually reminisced. I told her my whole story of searching, all the twists and turns, all the evidence I had gathered along the way. In between vignettes, I reveled in this time with my mother, feeling now life would be different. We would take this back with us. The twin saga would become an acknowledged piece of my history. We would carry it together. We would talk about it to others. We had healed together.

When it was almost time for my father to come out of surgery, we returned to the family waiting area. When we walked in, we both noticed that the movie playing on the TV was *Twins*, the spoof featuring Arnold Schwarzenegger and Danny DeVito as twins. We looked at each other and started laughing.

"If I ever do write about this, I can't put this in," I said. "No one would believe it."

I felt close to my mother that day and I know she felt close to me in a way we hadn't managed for a long time, if ever.

At the end of the day, as we drove home musing about

our experience together, my mother said to me, "You know, your father is right. You ARE an interesting person!"

Ah yes, my mother's specialty, the complex acknowledgment wrapped in rejection.

No matter. I had a mother for a day, and that was enough to fuel my heart for a long time to come.

I COULDN'T HAVE BEEN MORE WRONG IN THINKING THAT the day at the hospital with my mother during my father's surgery had solved everything - improving my relationship with her and vanquishing the belief that I was carrying the twin story alone. Everything we talked about that day simply fell back into the void, leaving me to wonder if I'd imagined it.

I went back to Boston and resumed my life.

One year later, I was again visiting my mother, and we were once again at a table in a restaurant having a meal. I thought of our last such conversation and decided to confirm not only that it had happened, but the conclusion we had drawn from it.

"Mom, I just want to go back to when we were at the hospital for Dad's surgery. I came away from our conversation that day thinking you had concluded there was a twin and Dad had concealed that knowledge from you. Is that what you were saying?" I asked.

"Yes, I'm afraid so," she said, then immediately raised

her hand to flag the waiter. "Could we have more bread, please?"

When she returned her attention to the table, she started talking about the latest events in her ongoing fury at my father since they'd separated.

Some months or even years after that lunch, I heard from my brother that our mother was back to, "How could Barb think I would give away a child?"

I was interviewed for a radio show about a screenplay I had written about the story and decided I should let her know, in case she heard about it, or in the event she had questions about it.

"I don't mind," she said. "Anyone who knows me knows I had nothing to do with it."

I never mentioned the story to my mother again. But on one memorable occasion, she brought it up.

When Gram, my maternal grandmother, had a bad fall and had to have emergency brain surgery, all the family gathered in Pittsburgh. I was one of the last to arrive, and by the time I got there, people were exhausted from their multi-day vigil, so my mother and aunt and other family members went home to rest, while I and my cousin's wife sat with Gram. A little after midnight, Gram passed away.

Early the next morning, as light was peaking over the horizon, I found my mother sitting quietly at the table in my grandmother's kitchen. I had come in very late from the hospital and hadn't seen my mother since Gram's death. I poured a cup of coffee and silently joined her at the table. We spoke a few words about Gram's passing and then my mother said, "I've been thinking about your twin. I guess we'll never know what really happened."

I took in what she'd said without responding. In those

still, quiet moments after her mother's passing, this was the last thing I imagined would be on my mother's mind, yet on another level it made perfect sense to me. Death has a way of gathering its accomplishments as a new member joins the other side. To that degree, I wouldn't have been surprised if my mother had brought up my cousin Rick's passing, or her brother Rich's passing from so long ago.

But my twin?

I knew this was a tiny, tenuous moment, such as when a hummingbird lands on the feeder and you want to observe, fearing the slightest movement will chase it away. I sat, hands around my mug, first looking into my mother's face and then respectfully nodding as I averted my gaze and sat in silence. It occurred to me that there are certain losses which are catalogued and stored in our hearts together and perhaps I was observing a *mother-daughter loss* connection-- that when my mother lost her own mother, she simultaneously experienced a loss she had experienced as a mother.

A moment of mystery. We never spoke of the twin again.

After they had been separated for fifteen years, my parents died within months of each other. My mother went first. She had been bitter about their break-up and had consistently rebuffed all of my father's efforts to reconnect with her in any form. A week before she died, she said, "I always loved him," and agreed to a telephone conversation with him. Although we children were in the house, we were careful not to listen in.

By the time my father died, he was living near me in

Boston. I had brought him to Massachusetts after my mother left Florida to live with my sister in Maryland. I wasn't able to accommodate him in my home as Joyce had with our mother. Instead, I found out an affordable assisted living nearby in Quincy. I visited the facility several times before I signed the papers, never knowing until the day I brought him in that I had been entering the place from the rear side of the building.

On his day of admission, we came through the front entrance. To our surprise (and my father's delight) we discovered the facility was next door to the very first Dunkin' Donuts, now not only an operating store but a historic landmark. I couldn't believe it. Maybe there was a God after all and he, she or it, granted our wishes in a way that was just right for us.

Because of my experience with my mother, I had completely let go of the twin story as far as my family was concerned. The week before my father died, he and I were driving back from a visit with his cardiologist, who had not had encouraging news. We were making our way through rush hour traffic back to his apartment, as Johnny Cash kept us entertained with *Ring of Fire*, one of my father's favorites which we had listened to over and over and over again when my brother and I drove our father from Florida to Massachusetts two years prior. Those chords and lyrics had become instant reminders of happy, even downright hilarious moments from that journey, and even in the Boston traffic jam, it had the capacity to transport us to a happier time. We sang along to the end of the song and then there was silence as I negotiated traffic before putting in another CD.

Suddenly, my father spoke.

"Remember when you thought you were a twin?" my father asked as he gave his little Yogi Bear chuckle. "You're over that now, aren't you?"

I wish I could report a kind and compassionate response—the one I'd imagined for years, which would take place as he took his last breath. Some version of this fantasy would have him confessing and me patting his hand and smiling benignly. Other versions were similar, but without any confession, me just being with him in a loving and present way with no need to have anything resolved one way or the other. My fervent wish was to allow my dad to leave this life feeling loved, unlike how he'd come in, and the opposite of the predominant tone of his life.

I guess I'd watched too many Hollywood movies. I was sure it would all come together in that last scene before he took his last breath, and I would be by his bedside holding his hand, nodding and letting him know I forgave him and all was well.

That's not what happened. I was taken aback by the question and yet I had to keep maneuvering the car in the rush hour traffic. His two questions scrambled my brain.

Remember when you thought you were a twin?

He spoke it through his signature smirk as though he was making fun of me, as though he were saying, "Remember when you believed in Santa Claus?: His phrasing and the question itself shocked my brain.

The context was reminiscent of how, through the years, he had only ever broached this subject when it was impossible for me to fully respond. The dinner with my grandmother and great aunt, the presenting of Kaye's birth certificate when my mother had been around and today, in traffic, as I was busy driving, after no conversation about this for years.

And then, the question....

You're over that now, aren't you?

Even though this took place in a nano-second, this exchange held our entire relationship. Something inside me got it instantly and completely. He was asking for absolution without ever having to acknowledge the sin.

It was a trap—conscious or not—an impossible and familiar manipulation that had spanned my whole life. It was as though he'd said to me, "Can I use the fact that I am dying in order to ease my burden without ever easing yours?"

Truth is, if it had happened in any other circumstance, like in the midst of a conversation, I think by then I would have been able to let it go. To essentially say with graciousness, "It's okay, Dad. Go in peace."

But that wasn't how it happened. As I negotiated my way onto the southeast expressway in rush hour traffic, the question seemed to suddenly fill the car, and a primitive part of my brain, or maybe it was my unfettered soul, simply spoke it's truth.

"No, Dad. That is the most important story of my life."

Any other response would have been an abandonment not only of myself in order to give privilege to my father's life and pain, it would also be abandoning Kaye.

He went silent. Neither of us spoke for the remainder of the ride back to his apartment.

And we never talked about it again.

CHAPTER 37

REFLECTIONS

IN THE END, I DON'T KNOW THE TRUTH.

I don't know in an outer, factual, provable way that Kaye was my twin.

I don't know if I had a twin who was someone other than Kaye.

I don't know if my father had a role in giving away my twin.

I do know two contradictory things:

- Even if Kaye was not my twin, there is nothing within me that could ever be convinced there was not a twin, any more than I could be convinced that my heart never beat. It is to this degree that I know the truth in my body.

-Even today, after all this searching, if, in fact, it were proven in the material world that there was a twin and she was given away, I would find it too heartbreaking to bear.

It took me years of shuttling back and forth between frantic searching and mindless disavowing to understand that neither of these realities was a feasible resting place for me.

I have learned, with the help of many others, to live my life in the in-between, holding the tension between is and is not, was and was not, because to step a millimeter in either direction, takes me to an insoluble dilemma.

Either:

There never was a twin, which means I've lived a totally delusional life, I've ruined my family and I can't trust my own knowing.

OR

There really was a twin and someone (maybe my father) gave her away, and my heart will never heal from that loss and betrayal.

This does not make sense to my analytical mind, which even now continues to search for answers. When it comes upon a nugget of information that could break my heart, it starts another excavation, and when that one leads to pain, it moves on, over and over again, just like Digger.

I don't know if my father was involved. If so, had he repressed this knowledge or was he merely maintaining a lie?

If so, did he have any choice given his upbringing? There was nothing in his life that ever taught him it was safe to make a mistake. He had never seen what forgiveness looked like, so he could never expect it. He was trying to survive.

Given the givens, my teenaged, children-of-alcoholic parents did a pretty good job. If I must pass judgment, I could wonder what an ungrateful brat I was to have made such a big deal of this. The privilege my parents provided me, above what they themselves ever had, gave me the perch upon which I could look back in judgment.

An unconscious ingrate.

On the other hand, what I feel in my bones is that I am

responsible for bringing consciousness to my own life, and I am responsible, to the extent I can, to be respectful and loving to others. Sometimes I think of the twin story, not as mine, although I am a central player, but as a karmic issue between my parents in which I was entangled. For years I had a recurrent image of having my skirt caught in the back door of a car in which my parents were sitting and about to pull away. Who could blame me for bringing it to their attention, getting them to stop the car so I could get to safety? Who would hold me responsible for ruining their trip?

Still, a part of me continues to defend itself.

I did not consciously seek out the story. If it wasn't in my DNA and in my deep unconscious, someone, presumably my mother, planted the information in plain sight for me to find while denying it in her own tissue. She is the one who told the fairy tale of Mrs. Wechsler's baby. I carried it until it told itself in the right circumstances at The Dinner Party.

Could I have chosen not to follow the lead? I tried. The pull was strong to protect what I had at the cost of knowing the truth.

After years of turning this over and over in my mind, it has been important for me to find my way out of the blame game. Our culture pulls for bifurcations, right/wrong, victim/perpetrator. Blame and punishment go hand-in-hand. Forgiveness is considered an optional nicety.

If I were to assign blame to someone, to anyone, who would it be?

My father and mother are obvious enough targets. Or would I blame my alcoholic grandfathers for not guiding their children? Or should I blame their upbringing, or the collective ignorance about addiction?

Should I blame the mine owner for the disaster that killed my great grandfather, leaving his sick wife to raise their four children, which led to my grandmother becoming an orphan at fifteen and a mother herself at sixteen?

Or maybe I should step across the ocean to Scotland and blame the terrible conditions there, as well as a family shame, that led my great-great grandfather to flee to the United States.

Blame is a very huge ball of yarn to try to unravel, and the easy, but unfair application of it is to just snip it off at the last infraction.

I refuse to entertain blame. I do feel sorrow and compassion for all parties in this story. We all hurt, and we all hurt each other. We all grow and love if we choose to. There is no avoiding these truths.

There are no villains and there are no saints.

The beauty of my life includes the puzzles of pain I have been given to solve, as well as the agony of separation, and it has created the yearning which can never be satisfied by an outer circumstance yet can fuel a heart for a lifetime.

I accept and forgive the imperfections and poor decisions of others and hope to uncover, accept and forgive the same in myself.

In the words of W.H Auden:

O stand, stand at the window
  As the tears scald and start
  You shall love your crooked neighbor
  With your crooked heart

CHAPTER 38

TWINSBURG, OHIO

EVEN AS I PULLED INTO THE PARKING LOT OF THE HILTON Garden Inn, I knew I was in a different universe. I saw a number of cars with duplicate people in various stages of unloading. Each car had its own set of adults dressed identically, getting out of the cars and unwittingly moving in unison. As I followed several pairs into the lobby, I felt strangely out of place. I watched from the line at the registration desk as each set approached the clerk. I listened in on what was a singular conversation conducted by two people talking either at once or simultaneously. When the clerk addressed one, the other answered, or completed an answer begun by his twin. The oddest part of all was that the clerk was nonplussed to have all his customers approaching the desk in two's. When it was my turn, I said my name.

"Is your sister or brother already here?"

For a second, I wondered why he would ask about Joyce and Bill, then I realized he thought I was a twin. He

ASSUMED I was a twin. It felt good. I didn't want to ruin the moment by explaining.

"No, not yet." I said.

As I took the suitcase out of my trunk, I wondered if this was such a good idea after all. The Annual Twins Festival in Twinsburg, Ohio is where every year thousands of twin sets from all over the world convene for a weekend of fun. It was where I had planned to come with Kaye the first August after we met, if we'd met. It sounded like a blast—lots of activities, games, competition (a three-legged race like you've never seen). There were organized events like golfing and a talent show, as well as many researchers who hoped to recruit twins for their studies. From the highway, I saw billboards and signs advertising two-for-one rates for everything from food to haircuts.

It felt right when I'd made the decision to go. After that ceremony of separation at Kripalu I'd felt at peace, not as *separate* as I would have expected, but integrated in a comfortable way within, ending the wrenching, frustrating search externally. In the meantime, my *twin within* found expression in amusing ways.

Several years after Kripalu, I travelled to a week-long program with Marion at a resort in Canada. When I arrived, a member of Marion's staff whom I'd never met approached me and introduced herself.

"There was a peculiar situation about your reservation, "she began. "It is resolved now but I wanted to ask you, is there any reason you would have reserved two rooms?"

She went on to tell me that the resort had reserved two rooms for me. The staff brought this to their attention, assuming it was in error, because the workshop needed the extra room. The resort insisted I had reserved two rooms. The staff member tried to explain that it didn't make sense for anyone to have two rooms, because each room had two beds and a desk. Besides, we would be in workshop about ten hours a day, so we would hardly be in the rooms except to sleep. The resort representative would not budge. The workshop coordinator had to call the registrar at UCLA who was handling administrative details and ask them to pull out my original application in order to confirm that I didn't reserve two rooms.

How amusing, I thought. "Does Marion know this happened?

"No," the assistant said.

"Tell her. See what she says."

Later that day I saw Marion.

She shook her head and laughed. "You certainly live an archetypal life."

I understood exactly. The *twin within*, the *lila*, continued to exist invisibly in my psyche, making appearances at unpredictable moments.

I'd argued with my impulse to go to the Twins Festival, assuming it would be a masochistic thing to do. After all, I had made peace with my family by taking my search into the inner world of the psychological and emotional and leaving it to them to find closure in their own ways. Why stir things up by going to Twinsburg?

On the other hand, the urge was so insistent, I wondered if my psyche was leading the way, even though I didn't consciously know why.

I threw my suitcase on the bed and looked around the room.

"So I'm here. What now?" I asked out loud.

The first event of the weekend was a parade which I didn't want to miss. I got up extra early and went to Denny's for breakfast. When the hostess greeted me as I reached the front of the line, she said, "Two?"

"No, just one," I answered.

As I followed her to a small booth in the corner, I pondered. Why did I have to say *just*", as if it was unusual, as if it was an apology. As I looked around and saw only two's, I realized I was unusual, as odd as if I'd said, "Yes, Just one shoe please. Yes, that's right, I'm only wearing one today." In this new world, people were among the items which usually only occurred in pairs.

As I settled into my booth, I looked up to see a mirror facing me. I smiled at the image looking back at me, then quickly looked around to make sure no one saw me smiling at myself. It was such a nice surprise. For a moment I could believe you were there looking back at me, dressed exactly like me. As I waited for my breakfast, I held up one of the brochures in front of me and from it, I silently read the history of the town to you.

A set of identical twins from Killingworth, Connecticut purchased some 4000 acres of land in 1819 and began selling small parcels at low prices to attract other settlers. The Wilcox twins then offered six acres of land for a public square and $20.00 toward starting the first school if the residents would change the settlement's name from Millsville to Twinsburg.

Isn't that a riot? Only $20 to wield such political influence that would last almost 200 years!

I looked around the room. I definitely was the only singleton. There were several tables of two and more tables of four or six. I had the impression that these larger tables were people who had met in prior years and had made a bond. Either that or there were a number of families with unusual numbers of multiples.

I felt comfortable, then odd for feeling comfortable. On one hand, this felt like a world to which I should belong, something that felt natural to me. On the other hand, I felt odd because I was alone, and unlike the others, I had no visible twin. I wondered what others thought of me sitting there alone and then I realized, why would they even notice?

I walked over to that public square that the Wiicox twins had so thoughtfully created, to find a good standpoint from which to watch the parade. The sidewalks were packed and there was a palpable excitement coming from each dyad I encountered.

The people were so absorbed! They were looking at each other and were enthusiastically engaged in conversation. I imagined perhaps these twins lived a distance from each other and were excited to be together for this event. However, in talking with them later, I learned they both lived in the same small town about an hour away from Twinsburg. They were just jazzed!

While we waited for festivities to begin, I met two women, one from Seattle and one from Georgia, who stood with their arms completely intertwined. They were beaming. They asked me where my twin was and I explained that she had died. Their faces, both of them, instantaneously fell flat, their eyes suddenly dead. They didn't ask any questions or offer any condolences, they simply turned and moved on.

I realized how mistaken I'd been that I would receive the understanding that wasn't available to me at the time you died, Kaye. Instead it felt as if I had just presented them with the most horrible scenario that they could ever imagine and they feared it was contagious. They didn't want to feel it, even for a second. From then on, when I met someone and they asked where my twin was I merely said she couldn't come and then switched the conversation to them.

The parade marshals (yes, of course there were two) began the festivities with a welcome. They talked about the history of Twinsburg and of course the history of the parade. They acknowledged their organizers and the town and then brought up a family of three sets of twins produced by two twin parents (not twins to each other), and they announced the winner for who had come the farthest, a set of men from Malaysia.

And then the tide began to roll. Hundreds of sets of identically dressed twins of all ages, all ethnicities, from a dozen countries, six or eight across, streamed past. At first it took my breath away and then it drew my tears. I can't say for what; they felt like tears of happy recognition, of being at home, mixed with tears of loss, an inner moment of rain and sunshine. I half expected a rainbow to appear around me.

After the parade, the waves of people headed toward the fairgrounds for the afternoon activities and food. After I downed a great-tasting, greasy kielbasa sandwich, I meandered through the vendor tents buying books either by twins or about twins, buying some silly trinkets with twin-related themes and one T-shirt.

Then my energy began to flag. My initial surprise and enjoyment of being in a sea of twins had felt great at first, but now that stiff, happy upper lip was quivering and my all-too-familiar sadness began pulling my cheeks to the asphalt. I was tired, but I was mostly sad and concerned that any minute, the emotional tsunami I'd thought was a thing of the past would catch up to me.

I passed a woman standing outside her booth passing out brochures. I took one eagerly, grateful to have something to focus my mind on other than my sadness. The brochure described Twin-to-Twin Transfusion syndrome, a fetal-threatening condition where one twin gets a disproportionate amount of nutrition in the womb. I had never heard of it and I did find it interesting. The woman herself had experienced that syndrome while carrying twin boys and had lost one of her sons as a result of it. She was passionate about spreading the word to help other women avoid her fate.

Looking into her sad eyes, I started to cry. She followed suit by tearing up. We stood silently for a moment, each of us wiping away a tear and waiting for composure to reassert itself. We smiled into a half-laugh.

"I'm Marcy," she said.

She went on to tell me more about her experience and the experience of her surviving son, who had just turned ten. When she saw me tear up again, she gently asked, "Do you have twins? Or did you lose twins?"

I paused, not sure what to say. "No. I believe I am a twin and my twin was given away at birth."

"Oh!" she softly gasped. "That is so painful."

She went on to tell me how her son had suffered from the loss of his twin in utero.

"It's more complicated than you would think. Many parents believe the surviving twin should not be told their twin died in utero, assuming they would not know this on their own. But new research shows otherwise. Memory exists before birth, especially for twins. Twins begin life by reacting, before thinking even develops, to the energy of touch, and to the rhythm of shared heartbeats, in addition to those shared with the mother. They create little memory capsules called engrams ..." she looked up at me and seemed to recognize I wasn't completely following.

She was right. My mind and brain were taking it in, but my emotions were doing their own sorting and filing.

She pulled back. "If you are interested, here is a list of resources on this

topic. The take away is that twins do remember, but because the experience happens before conscious thought is developed, the memory is stored in the body, so to speak."

"When did your son learn he had a twin who died in utero?"

"We told him in second grade, once we understood what was happening, but I think that was late. He was a loner. He never felt as if he were part of the group. Once we told him, it had an almost immediate impact on his personality. He still felt different, but he had a reason for it and he was proud of his uniqueness. Of course, there was and still is another side to it,"

My head was swimming. With just the little Marcy had told me, I began to see my situation in a different light. Yes, being in the womb as a twin had memory traces, and yes, if I heard her correctly, she'd confirmed that the truth IS in the body.

"Most of my knowledge is within the framework of Twin-to-Twin Transfusion so I don't know about twins separated later. But there is a group called Twinless Twins International. Here is a brochure about them. It's for those who experience twin separation at any time in life and under any circumstance. It's been helpful for me in understanding Joey better."

This was so interesting. No, it was more than that. It was impactful--so much so I felt as if I was going to shut down, fall asleep on my feet.

"Thank you, Marcy," I said. "I'll follow up on your suggestion."

CHAPTER 39

BRINGING IT HOME

I WAS HAPPY TO BE BACK HOME.

I had wondered about the synchronicity of my going to Twinsburg right at the time Ruth's parents were visiting. At first, I thought this meant I should not go, but in the end, I went, realizing they would like nothing better than to be alone with Ruth for a weekend. It never dawned on me that another important reason to go would be for Ruth's father, Norbert.

Norbert is a Twinless Twin. His brother Normand died of rheumatic fever when they were nineteen years old. It was a while after I was with Ruth, perhaps when I first told her my own twin story, that she told me her father is a twin. Even then, it struck me that people are drawn to each other for reasons they don't even know until they are together awhile and discover a core similarity, a nugget of their histories that match up like puzzle pieces. Twin loss was the hidden, unresolved seed between Ruth and I. me

Ruth said her father never talked about his twin so she, her sister and her mother knew very little about him or the circumstances of his death. They knew the basic facts but not anything about Norbert's feeling or his relationship with his brother.

A few months after meeting Ruth's parents, they came to visit and had some old family photos that they had retrieved from their hometown in Vermont which they were going to take back to Florida to restore. As we looked through the photographs, without thinking, I made conversation with Norbert about the photos of him and his brother. I felt Ruth and her mother holding their breath through this part of the conversation, as Norbert haltingly told me about Normand. Later Ruth told me she had no memory of her father ever talking about Normand and it was a topic no one in the family ever broached with him.

Over time, as I have become involved in unearthing my own story, there have been many conversations around the dining table about Kaye, beginning, of course, with my telling them the entire story. Norbert was always a very active participant in these conversation about my lost twin, never referring to his own experience. He began to take an active role in making suggestions for tactics I might take to locate records. Last summer he supplied me with contact information for Florida agencies which might help me.

So it shouldn't have been hard for me to realize that my going to Twinsburg, Ohio in the midst of their visit, was a synchronous event that would have impact on Norbert, and on Ruth's family.

I came back from the weekend amidst complications of travel which greatly diluted my re-entry report. My flight back was canceled and I had to spend an additional night in Cleveland. During the drive home from Providence airport, my car broke down and I had to wait for two and a half hours for a tow truck that never came. The end result was that my car was totally unsalvageable and I had to immediately launch into getting it replaced. Even with those exigencies, my spirit was undaunted. I'd come back with an unshakable equanimity and I talked about my experiences. I talked about the parade of thousands of twins, about individual encounters, about becoming acquainted with the Twinless Twin network. At every telling, they were a quiet but attentive audience.

Then a few days after I was home, the four of us took the afternoon and went up to the North Shore. We walked along the beach in Gloucester, we visited shops in Rockport and then we headed on over to Essex for a meal at *Wood-man's in the Rough*, a favorite rustic gathering place for deliciously-bad-for-you fried seafood as well as lobster.

While in Gloucester, we went into a café for a beer and to wait out a rain squall. Something opened in Norbert and he began talking about his brother Normand. He told stories of their childhood, told of the attention people paid them because they were twins. How they were fraternal twins and did not look alike. Normand, the firstborn, was sickly his whole life and was always smaller than Norbert. Nevertheless, people couldn't remember who was who, perhaps because their names were so similar.

As he talked, I noticed how alert and attentive both Ruth and her mother were to Norbert's tale.

As we left the North Shore in the early dusk to drive the one hour back to Boston, Norbert, from the back seat, began to tell more tales of him and Normand. He told about how smart Normand was.

"He was the smart one, I was the dumb one."

I found this surprising, given that Norbert is a very

intelligent, if not educated man. He told how he went into the service and would send half of his paycheck home to pay for Normand's college. I asked if that was because it was expected or because he wanted to.

"Oh, I wanted to," he replied..

He told about how Normand was in the Lahey Clinic, brought to the Boston area from Vermont for treatment. Norbert remembered coming up from the South where he was stationed in the Navy to visit Normand there shortly before he died.

It was special to hear Norbert talk about his twin. I reflected on the unspoken bond I felt with Norbert which probably had always emanated from this shared history, whether it had been made explicit or not. This theme of the twin was so apparent in Ruth's history, even though it was never talked about. Ruth and her sister were born just thirteen months apart, and in all practical ways they were raised like twins--they dressed alike and they were treated equally. Norbert spent a lot of time playing with them, building an ice-skating rink in the back yard, taking them on snow-mobiles and out fishing. Ruth and Lynn are about as close to being twins as two can be without actually being twins.

The next evening as we prepared to go to bed, Ruth said to me, "Wasn't that amazing the way my father talked about Normand?" She was clearly affected by Norbert's disclosure. "He has never told us anything about all that."

I smiled, thinking that in its way, despite our various resistances, that old Twinless Twin network had reached out and touched two for one.

CHAPTER 40

TWINLESS TWINS REVISITED

IN THE WEEKS FOLLOWING MY RETURN FROM THE TWINS Festival, I followed up on Marcy's suggestions for learning more about twinless twins.

Page after page validated my experience of life more completely than anything I had learned, or studied or been treated for, because no one had been able to validate for me what my own inner life had been showing me. For the first time, I didn't need to seek outside for someone to give me myself, to tell me whether or not I was a twin. I had been given specific knowledge which pointed to the truth that was indeed in my body--so that I could recognize myself, so I could become whole.

This feeling is reminiscent of the moment in my search when I was desperate to experience what it would have been like to have lived with my twin.

Ruth, a graphic designer, altered a favorite photo of me, in which my head is at an angle. She duplicated the image, switched it around and pasted it in close to the original so it looked as if the two heads are tilted in towards each other.

Kind of looked like the twin cows, come to think of it. At first sight of the photo, I thought, *"That's what I look like,"* not, *"That's what WE look like."* What *I* look like.

The two of us, a singular thing. I framed that picture and kept in on the piano for years. Seeing it, I felt whole.

As I spent time with the Twinless Twin material, I was astonished by the very specific descriptions I found, so many of which I had experienced, while other materials explained some of my character or personality traits.

-- *When an individual discovers he has lost a twin at birth, it can be traumatic...In every case, however, there is one startling moment when intellectual and emotional awarenesses suddenly meld, yielding a blast of insight. The twin discovers one who does not exist in tangible form. He finds a person who must remain forever missing. The confusion is reported to be stunning.*

Yes! This was what had happened to me after The Dinner Party!

-- *The loss of an identical twin has been shown to elicit a more intense grief reaction than that of any other relative.*

So I am not crazy, histrionic or delusional to have fallen apart at Kaye's death!

– *For many twinless twins, birthdays are an unsettling time. It is the most dark and depressing day of the year and they prefer to be left alone with their thoughts and feelings. They feel overwhelmed with physical pain.*

All those scowling birthday photos of me and Mom.

-- *Surviving twins constantly strive to demonstrate their autonomy and completeness.*

This one makes me laugh. I feel anyone who knows me nodding their heads. If I'd been shot in the back and someone asked me how I was, I'm sure I'd say "Finethanky-ouandyou."

-- Twinless twins are protective of their parents, unconsciously trying to be the good twin.

Oy...

-- Twinless twins fear not being believed or thought of as strange or weird.

I was devastated when a family therapy professor called me an odd duck.

-- Twinless twins report an interior dialog with their twin. A private world where the only other is privy to one's intimate thoughts and emotions. It is reported that this internal dialogue goes on for a lifetime and is best understood only by other twinless twins.

So what do you think of this one, Kaye? Elvis was a twinless twin from birth, and he never told anyone that he talked constantly to Jesse until he was 28 years old.

-- The incidence of separation and divorce among surviving twins is four times that of singletons. The reason is basic: they have already been spoken for in the relationship with their twin...an image of an already achieved, intense and unconditional commitment. Frida Kahlo was married to a twinless twin, Diego Rivera, and she said of him, "He's not really anybody's husband, if you want to be with him, you simply accept him."

Sorry to anyone who's tried to be with me, I never knew that place next to me was already taken.

I recognize it is the task of all of beings, maybe not just humans, to individuate, to find life separate from any other. Twins are not exempt. It is easy to romanticize the perfection of the twin bond as I have done for my entire life. But I know, if we had grown up together, we would have had our own struggles about individuating from each other in order to establish our separate identities, to become who we really are.

I've come to understand that twins come to earth with

their own special context. Research has shown the twin bond to each other can be stronger than to the mother, and in fact, that twins reared by a mentally ill mother fare better than singletons in similar circumstances. Twins have their own context, and when the dyad is not present it can affect their development. It's as if twins have their own specialized boxing ring where they work it out together. The twinless twin material helped me to see my human challenges in a different light—it is as if I was wired for that ring but have been alone in it without my sparring partner. Being the only one in the ring spawns a life of waiting for someone who never comes, of no wins and no losses. The only option for growth is to step out of the ring.

And no matter how bonded, twins generally leave the world individually (unless they are conjoined like Chang and Eng and even then, there was gap of hours). We can't avoid our encounter with separation.

Ironically, I felt much less lonely once I read the material on twinless twins. I felt understood and my life made more sense. For me, it was an experience of finding rather than losing.

All my digging, looking inside for confirmation of my connection to Kaye became my connection to Kaye, as real to me, and as ineffable as my connection to my own self and to that Nameless Knower.

I have found the deeper I go, there is no such thing as a twinless twin, there is only Presence, the presence from which we emerged and presumably into which we will one day dissolve.

Oneness.

That's what we all look like.

ACKNOWLEDGEMENTS

THERE IS A SPECIAL NIGHTMARE THAT ACCOMPANIES THE completion of a memoir, especially when it is a story one has been trying to tell for twenty years or more, and that anxiety has to do with acknowledgements. "What if I forget someone?"

There are those who had vital roles in my story whom I can't directly thank, either because they have passed on or because I never got their full names; two examples of this respectively are the late Marion Woodman and the late Anne Craffey, my roommate and hostess of The Dinner Party, as well Kim, the woman from Jacksonville who mistook me for Kaye and whose last name I never knew. There are many others who have held this story with me in a number of ways, from those who heard the story over the dining table once, to those who have heard it in the context of their professional role with me, and still others who have been with me, day in and day out for years, encouraging me every step of the way. I am deeply grateful to every single one of you!

I hope it goes without saying that I feel a deep gratitude for people you've met in the pages of this book who became the companion "other" that helped me to take my search to the end. Olivia Hoblitzelle, my official "task companion" came into my life at the precise moment when I was ready to move into action. In the last twenty-five years, she and I have had dinner together once a month; even allowing for four missed dates per year for vacation or holiday, that comes to over two hundred meals together! And we have never run out of vital topics for discussion. This book has her influence on every page. Caroline Marvin, my teacher and mentor, is the heroine who showed up at a number of points in the story as well as in my life, just when I needed her. Caroline, I will be forever grateful. Peter Faust, the Barbara Brennan healer, appeared at a dramatically low moment and it was he who steadfastly challenged me by saying, "You must do something. This will never go away." Thank you, Peter, without your guidance, I might still be spinning my wheels!

I thank my family who have been a part of this story from the beginning: my mother and father, my sister Joyce Flick and my brother Bill McCollough as well as the Western Pennsylvanian relatives: my grandparents, my aunts, uncles and cousins, who, whether they explicitly knew the story or not, have loved and nourished me throughout my life. A special thank you goes to Kathi Miller, my father's youngest sister, one year older than I, who I think of as my "aunt-cousin and alternate twin sister". To my family by marriage: Norbert and Monique Lague, Lynn, Claire, and Breisja Jennings, thank you not only for your contribution to this book but also to my life!

In addition, my life has been blessed with 'families of

choice", those who have carried this story with me and for me over many years whether in a social context, as school friends, and as participants in writing or book groups, or psychospiritual development programs. Listed here according to the phase of the story's unfoldment from thirty years ago up to the present are:

- Ron Bachman, Jenni Dilworth, BJ Entwisle, Julie Marston, Jane McInerny, Amy Podolsky
- Pamela Gerloff, Connie Haskell, Sasha Katz, Gitte Kushner, Peg Lorenz, Leah Neuchiller
- Merle Bicknell, Ruth Davidson, Jackie Gelb, Cinny Little, Amy Rossiter, Emily Sherwood, Christine Thurston
- Elizabeth Buck, Barbara Bunting, Barbara Ohrstrom, Sally Romoser

A current family of choice waits to move across the finish line with me. I can't express what it means to have had your interest, support and love in this endeavor. Thank you, Deborah Abel. Lee Perlman and Caleb Perlman, Sue Ellen Beers and Jill Tyzack, Karen and Gretchen Browne-Courage, Colleen Byrnes and Darcy Johnson, Jess Butler, Barbara (Bebe) Clark, Nicolas Despo and Karuna O'Donnell, Marsha Firestone, Julie Gabis and Karen Kulp, Kavita Hunt and Cheryl Harrell, Lorna Lyons, Jane McInerny, Claire McManus, Reggie Odom, and Sue Tracy. You all have been a precious part of this adventure!

Thank you to Luke Ferdinands, David Hipshman, Seth Levine, Bill Mueller, Monique Pommier, and Melanie Hahn Roche for helping me to stay connected to mind, body and spirit through the writing of this tale.

Then there are those who I think of as my "creative helpers" who have been closely associated with this story at different times and in different ways. Thank you to Lawrence Kessenich and Deborah Bluestein for providing supportive, safe environments via your writing groups where I began to find my own writing voice. Deep appreciation to Richard Hoffman whose ability to instill belief in his students while offering constructive feedback was an art in itself and has had a lasting impact not only on this story but on my development as a writer. Deep appreciation to both Caroline Heller and Amy Ellis Nutt who, through their work and 'generous genius' inspire me every day.

Many thanks to Baeth Davis, Life Purpose Coach, who challenged me to turn my story into a screenplay. Thank you, group members Barbara Cotta, Marilyn Deluca, Helene Desruisseaux, Sherry Green, Holly Martin, Sharon Moist and Reggie Odom for being my first readers. This experience led to a collaboration with Hollywood producers Melora Hardin and Gildart Jackson (the screenplay referred to in the book). Thank you Melora and Gildart for your brilliant input.

I would be remiss in not mentioning the support that has made it possible for me to take the document from my computer into your hands as a book. Thank you to Kate Tilton and Edward Giordano, author's assistants, to Debra Kastner for editorial help, and Michelle Samplin-Salgado of Red Sofa Design for the book's cover and website design.

If you are still with me, you might be wishing there was a music conductor to 'play me off the page' like they do for Oscar winners who take too long on the stage offering appreciations. I understand their dilemma. If I never have this 'podium' again, I want to thank everyone who has been a part of the book coming into being. I could go back to Mrs. Applegate in the third grade but I have to stop somewhere! Apologies to Mrs. Applegate and others.

In closing, I offer special thanks to two prolific writers and stellar teachers, J.Thorn and Rachael Herron, co-hosts of *The Writer's Well* podcast. I had the good fortune of working with J. as a Certified Story Grid Editor who helped me to structure my tale to make the story work and then with Rachael Herron who became my developmental editor, contributing her generous heart and careful pen to the project. I can truly say without J. and Rachael this book would not be in your hands. Thank you both from the bottom of my heart.

And to Ruth, my very own Frida Kahlo, I thank you for understanding and accepting me as I am, for living the story with me as it unfolded in all its tumultuous emotional turning , and then for supporting me through it all again as I tried to capture the story on the page. Your presence in my life is a profound treasure.

ABOUT THE AUTHOR

BARBARA McCOLLOUGH is a psychotherapist, coach, mentor and consultant who has worked in a variety of organizational settings, as well as in private practice, for over thirty years. Her current passion is helping people to find and live the truest expression of themselves in the second half of life.

This is her first book.

BarbaraMcCollough.com

Made in the USA
Middletown, DE
30 December 2019